D1716630

GRIZZLY BEARS

Guardians of the Wilderness

FRANCES BACKHOUSE

ORCA BOOK PUBLISHERS

Text copyright © Frances Backhouse 2023

Published in Canada and the United States
in 2023 by Orca Book Publishers.
orcabook.com

All rights reserved. No part of this publication may be reproduced
or transmitted in any form or by any means, electronic or
mechanical, including photocopying, recording or by any
information storage and retrieval system now known or to be
invented, without permission in writing from the publisher.

Library and Archives Canada Cataloguing in Publication
Title: Grizzly bears : guardians of the wilderness /
Frances Backhouse.
Names: Backhouse, Frances, author.
Series: Orca wild ; 10.
Description: Series statement: Orca wild ; 10 |
Includes bibliographical references and index.
Identifiers: Canadiana (print) 20220210551 |
Canadiana (ebook) 20220210578 |
ISBN 9781459828544 (hardcover) | ISBN 9781459828551 (PDF) |
ISBN 9781459828568 (EPUB)
Subjects: LCSH: Grizzly bear—Juvenile literature. |
LCSH: Grizzly bear—Conservation—Juvenile literature.
Classification: LCC QL737.C27 B23 2023 | DDC j599.784—dc23

Library of Congress Control Number: 2022935250

Summary: This nonfiction book introduces middle-grade readers
to grizzly bears. Featuring photos throughout, it discusses
the bears' biology, habitats and threats to survival, and how
scientists, conservationists and young people are working
to protect grizzly populations.

Orca Book Publishers is committed to reducing the
consumption of nonrenewable resources in the production
of our books. We make every effort to use materials that
support a sustainable future.

Orca Book Publishers gratefully acknowledges the
support for its publishing programs provided by the following
agencies: the Government of Canada, the Canada Council
for the Arts and the Province of British Columbia through
the BC Arts Council and the Book Publishing Tax Credit.

The author and publisher have made every effort to
ensure that the information in this book was correct
at the time of publication. The author and publisher
do not assume any liability for any loss, damage, or
disruption caused by errors or omissions. Every effort has
been made to trace copyright holders and to obtain their
permission for the use of copyrighted material. The
publisher apologizes for any errors or omissions and would
be grateful if notified of any corrections that should be
incorporated in future reprints or editions of this book.

Front and back cover photos by John E. Marriott,
wildernessprints.com
Design by Jenn Playford
Edited by Kirstie Hudson

Printed and bound in South Korea.

26 25 24 23 • 1 2 3 4

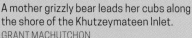

A mother grizzly bear leads her cubs along
the shore of the Khutzeymateen Inlet.
GRANT MACHUTCHON

To the Khutzeymateen grizzly bears who let me travel safely through their home for five months, put up with my curiosity and taught me so much about their lives.

CONTENTS

3
IT'S A BEAR'S LIFE

5
GRIZZLY BEARS AND YOU

4
CONSERVATION IN ACTION

A young Khutzeymateen grizzly bear munches on grasslike sedges. Greens are an important part of the springtime diet of all grizzlies.
FRANCES BACKHOUSE

INTRODUCTION

The hardest job I've ever had was studying grizzly bears. It was also one of the best. For five months I worked with two other biologists in a remote wilderness area on British Columbia's north coast called the Khutzeymateen. This area is located in Ts'msyen territory and the name comes from the Sm'algya̱x language, spoken by the Ts'msyen People. The Sm'algya̱x spelling for Khutzeymateen is K'ts'imadiin—a word that means "head of the inlet where the two rivers meet, in the valley."

The other biologists and I were there to collect information about where the grizzlies traveled, what they ate and where they fed, slept and left messages for each other by rubbing against trees. But we couldn't just go out and hope to stumble across them. To keep tabs on the bears we captured a few and put radio collars on them before releasing them. We tracked the signals that the collars sent out. Then we went to sites where the bears had been and collected information about their activities.

Here I am writing notes while doing grizzly-bear research in the Khutzeymateen. Fallen trees like the one I'm standing on help biologists and bears get above the dense vegetation on the forest floor.
FRANCES BACKHOUSE

There are no roads in the valley, so the river was our highway. We regularly had to get out and drag our boat through the shallows or cut away logs that blocked the channel. I often ended up with boots full of icy water. On land, we bushwhacked through the dense, wet rainforest and clambered up and down steep hillsides, carrying our heavy equipment on our backs.

By the time we returned to camp in the late afternoon, I was usually exhausted. But we still had to clean up and get organized for the next day. In the evenings we hunched over our notebooks and maps, building a picture of Khutzeymateen grizzly-bear life.

One of the greatest rewards of that job was that I got to spend so much time around wild grizzly bears. Hardly a day went by when I didn't spot at least one, and they were often so close that I didn't need binoculars to tell what they were up to. I'll never forget the two teenaged bear brothers who liked to slide down the snowy avalanche chute across from our camp or the times I watched cubs wrestling while their mother relaxed nearby.

This 33-year-old grizzly bear is nearing the end of his life. In 1990 I knew him as a four-year-old nicknamed Spanky. He and his brother, Wheezer, liked sliding on snow patches that lingered on the steep slopes above the inlet.
GRANT MACHUTCHON

A few years later I got an even bigger reward. In 1992 the British Columbia government decided that there must be no logging of the Khutzeymateen's old-growth forests because it would be too harmful to grizzly bears. In 1994 they sealed the deal by creating the Khutzeymateen/ K'tzim-a-deen Grizzly Bear Sanctuary—the first place in Canada protected specifically for grizzlies. I felt proud to have played a part in making that happen.

Keeping company with grizzly bears like I did that summer isn't for everyone. But you don't have to meet one face-to-face to understand what makes it special. This book gives you a chance to learn about grizzlies from people who have spent years getting to know them and working to make the world a better place for these guardians of the wilderness.

Me on the left with fellow biologists Stefan Himmer and Grant MacHutchon, working quickly to put a radio collar on a tranquilized grizzly bear. Once the bear is up and moving again, we will track the location signals sent out by the collar.
BILL JACKSON

A grizzly bear strolls through
a sea of sagebrush.
JIM PEACO/YELLOWSTONE NATIONAL PARK/
FLICKR.COM/PUBLIC DOMAIN

1
BRUIN
BASICS

THE HORRIBLE NORTHERN BEAR

Grizzly bears belong to a *species* known in English as the brown bear. Scientists call the brown bear *Ursus arctos*, which means "northern bear" in Latin. But brown bears aren't just northerners. They are the world's most widespread bears and once lived as far south as Egypt and Morocco. They are no longer found in Africa but still live in North America, Europe, Asia and the Middle East.

Brown bears are not exactly the same all over the world. Because of these differences, scientists divide the species into smaller groups called *subspecies*. It's like they're all on the same team—Team Brown Bear—but each one plays the game of life in its own unique way. Each subspecies gets a three-part scientific name made up of the species name plus a third word that uniquely identifies it. The grizzly bear's three-part name is *Ursus arctos horribilis*. Horribilis! It's a good thing bears don't understand Latin.

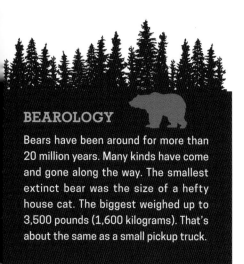

BEAROLOGY

Bears have been around for more than 20 million years. Many kinds have come and gone along the way. The smallest extinct bear was the size of a hefty house cat. The biggest weighed up to 3,500 pounds (1,600 kilograms). That's about the same as a small pickup truck.

Bruin means "brown" in the Dutch language. In the Middle Ages, it was used as a nickname for brown bears in folk tales and later became a common way to refer to all kinds of bears.
YATHIN S KRISHNAPPA/WIKIMEDIA COMMONS/ CC BY-SA 3.0

When naturalist George Ord gave the grizzly bear that scientific name back in 1815, he thought "horribilis" was an accurate description. But Ord had never actually met a grizzly bear. He had just read exaggerated descriptions of their fierceness written by other people who had never met a grizzly bear. One of those reports called grizzly bears "the enemy of man." It also claimed they had such a "thirst for human blood" that they would take any chance to attack people and even hunt them down.

That does sound pretty horrifying, but we now know better. While grizzlies are dangerous under certain circumstances, they would rather steer clear of humans than tangle with them. Horrible northern bear? Not at all. Just sometimes misunderstood.

ONE BEAR, MANY NAMES

The grizzly bear also has many other names. Its Indigenous names are as diverse as the people whose languages they come from. In the far north, Inuit call this bear akłak. On the Great Plains, Nakoda speakers know it as waȟ'ą kšija. And on the northwest coast its Tlingit name is xóots. Those are just some of the dozens of ways you can say "grizzly bear" as you travel around North America.

The first non-Indigenous people who encountered these bears were European explorers, fur traders and missionaries. They came up with their own word for this unfamiliar animal, but they took a while to agree on the spelling. Variations included *grisley beare*, *grissle bear* and *grizzle bear*. Eventually they settled on *grizzly bear* as the official English name. The word *grizzly* means "flecked or streaked with gray." When used for bears, it refers to their fur.

BROWN BEAR
• Lives in northwestern North America, northern Europe and Asia and parts of the Middle East.

• Uses a wider range of habitats than any other bear, including rainforests, grasslands and tundra.

AMERICAN BLACK BEAR
• Lives throughout Canada, much of the United States and parts of northern Mexico, mostly in forested areas.

• North America's most common bear.

POLAR BEAR
• The world's largest bear. Males can weigh up to 1,760 pounds (800 kilograms).

• Lives in Arctic regions all around the world, mostly out on the sea ice.

• Its thick white fur provides excellent insulation and camouflage.

BEARS AROUND THE WORLD
There are eight bear species worldwide. The three found in North America are the brown bear, the American black bear and the polar bear.

ANDEAN BEAR
• Lives in a wide range of habitats in the Andes Mountains in South America.

• Also known as the spectacled bear because it often has a circle or semicircle of white fur around each eye, making it look as if it's wearing spectacles.

ASIATIC BLACK BEAR
• Lives in forested areas in hills and mountains across southern Asia and in southeastern Russia and Japan.

• In fall often builds leafy feeding platforms in nut trees.

GIANT PANDA
• Lives in mountain forests in China.

• Eats almost nothing but bamboo and spends 10 to 12 hours each day feeding.

SLOTH BEAR
• Lives in dry forests and grasslands in India, Sri Lanka, Bangladesh, Nepal and Bhutan.

• After digging into ant or termite mounds, it sucks up its prey with its large, flexible lips.

SUN BEAR
• The world's smallest bear, weighing 60-145 pounds (27-65 kilograms).

• Lives in tropical rainforests in Southeast Asia.

• Uses its very long tongue to extract insects from tree crevices and honey from hives.

BEAR ILLUSTRATIONS: MAQUILADORA/SHUTTERSTOCK.COM

This bear's long claws and shoulder hump are sure signs that it is a grizzly. The curved line of its snout from eyes to nose tip is another good clue to its identity.
GRANT MACHUTCHON

Grizzly bears come in various colors. Shades of brown are the most common, ranging from deep chocolate to blond. Some grizzlies are so dark that they look black. Occasionally they are white. All grizzlies have long **guard hairs**, and the ends of those hairs are often pale, giving their coats a grizzled appearance. When light falls on their fur at certain angles, they look grayish or frosty or silvery. The Spanish name for the grizzly bear is el oso plateado, which translates as "the silver bear" in English. A popular English nickname for grizzlies is Silvertip.

In Alaska grizzlies are usually called brown bears, no matter what color their fur is. That can get confusing, so in this book I refer to those Alaskan bears as grizzly bears.

Whatever we call these bears, they are wondrous animals. They are massive and mysterious and have been stirring the human imagination since the dawn of time. Sometimes our feelings about them are focused on fear, and we treat them as enemies. But when we take time to know and understand them, respect can take the place of fear and grow into admiration and appreciation.

A brown mother grizzly bear shares a salmon with her blond cub. Blond or white grizzly bears are rare.
JOHN E. MARRIOTT, WILDERNESSPRINTS.COM

GRIZZLY BEAR

☐ Current Range

■ Lost Range

Grizzly bears used to live throughout the green and purple-colored areas on this map. They are now found only in the green areas. DATA ADAPTED FROM USGS - INTERAGENCY GRIZZLY BEAR STUDY TEAM. PUBLIC DOMAIN.

WHERE GRIZZLIES ROAM

Long ago the grizzly bear's homelands covered nearly half of North America. From north to south, grizzlies roamed from the shores of the Arctic Ocean all the way down to central Mexico. From west to east, their range stretched from the Pacific Coast to Hudson Bay and far out onto the Great Plains. They also lived in a small part of northern Quebec and Labrador called the Ungava Peninsula.

Today grizzly bears live in far fewer places. They have disappeared from about one-quarter of the area they used to inhabit in Canada. They are also gone from 94 percent of their former territory in the *Lower 48 states*—which is the part of the United States that lies between Canada and Mexico. And they are completely missing from Mexico.

Whether grizzly bears gain or lose ground in the future will largely depend on whether we are willing to rise to the challenges of coexistence, or living together.

The wide gap between the toe prints and claw marks in this track show that it was made by a grizzly bear. Black bears have shorter claws, so the toe prints and claw marks in their tracks almost touch.
GLACIER BAY NATIONAL PARK AND PRESERVE/NPS PHOTO

One of the roughly 3,500 bears that live on the Kodiak islands in Alaska. That's a density of about 0.7 bears per square mile (2.6 square kilometers).
LAURA HEDIEN/SHUTTERSTOCK.COM

KODIAK COUSINS

The grizzly bear's closest cousins live on the Kodiak islands in Alaska. These bears are commonly known as Kodiaks. They are usually considered to be a unique subspecies of brown bear called *Ursus arctos middendorffi*. But some biologists say Kodiaks are the same as grizzlies. It will take more research to settle the question.

Kodiak bears have lived apart from all other brown bears for 12,000 years. Forty miles (64 kilometers) of icy ocean waters keep the Kodiaks from crossing over to mainland Alaska and keep mainland grizzlies from visiting the Kodiak islands. Both groups of bears can swim, but not that far.

The most distinctive thing about Kodiak bears is that they're huge. They can weigh up to 1,500 pounds (680 kilograms) and stand about 5 feet (1.5 meters) tall at the shoulder. When the largest Kodiaks rise up on their hind legs, they tower more than 10 feet (3 meters) tall. You would need to stand on a friend's shoulders to look an upright Kodiak bear in the eye.

GRIZZLY-BEAR FEATURES

Even if you have never seen a bear in real life, you probably know what one looks like. But how can you tell if it's a grizzly bear?

In areas that are home to both grizzlies and American black bears, people often get the two confused because both can be black or brown or occasionally white.

The most noticeable differences between the two species are body shape and claw length. Grizzly bears have a bulky shoulder hump and very long front claws. American black bears have no shoulder hump and fairly short front claws.

There are also differences in the shape of the face and ears, but they aren't always obvious. If you look at a grizzly bear's head from the side, the area between the eyes and the tip of the nose looks concave or saucer-shaped. A black bear's face has a straight profile. Grizzly bears tend to have short, rounded ears. Black bears have taller, more triangular ears.

Size is the least reliable way to tell black bears and grizzlies apart, especially if they aren't standing side by side. American black bears are generally smaller than grizzlies, but a large black bear can outweigh a small grizzly bear.

The size of grizzly bears varies widely depending on their age and sex and where they live. Adult males that live in *inland* areas average around 430 pounds (195 kilograms). In coastal areas they occasionally top 1,000 pounds (454 kilograms) but average 650 pounds (295 kilograms). Adult females are about two-thirds of the weight of adult males in their area.

BEAROLOGY

The grizzly bear's shoulder hump is created by its huge shoulder muscles. Those muscles—combined with its long front claws—give grizzlies power and strength for digging up food, excavating winter dens and grappling with large prey.

A mother grizzly bear tears meat from a caribou carcass by the Toklat River in Alaska while her cubs play nearby.
EMILY MESNER/NPS PHOTO

A grizzly bear makes its way across the tundra. Fall frost has turned the leaves of the low shrubs bright red and gold.
JOHN E. MARRIOTT, WILDERNESSPRINTS.COM

FROM OCEANSIDE TO MOUNTAINTOP AND BEYOND

The place where an animal lives and can get all the things it needs to survive is called its *habitat*. Grizzly bears live in different types of habitat in different parts of North America. In coastal areas near the ocean their habitat includes forests, mudflats, beaches and rocky shorelines. In the Rockies and other mountainous areas, they ramble from valley bottoms to high ridges and peaks. Grizzlies of the far north are mostly found on the treeless *tundra*.

Grizzly bears have been pushed out of some other habitats that used to provide them with good homes. These include most of the grasslands in the middle of the continent and desert canyons and river valleys in the southwestern United States and northern Mexico.

No matter where grizzly bears live, they need lots of space. Each bear has its own *home range*. This is the area where it travels over the course of a year as it searches for food, mates, shelter and anything else it requires.

Two young grizzly bears find their balance just above the high-tide line. There's lots to eat here, including knobby barnacles attached to the rocks and crabs hiding beneath the seaweed.
EDDY SAVAGE/SHUTTERSTOCK.COM

Grizzlies don't treat their home ranges like private property where no other bear can set foot. In fact, their home ranges often overlap. But grizzlies mostly avoid being in the same place as other grizzlies at the same time.

A grizzly bear's home range consists of all the areas where it carries out different activities plus the travel routes that connect them. If you mapped out your own home range, it would probably include your kitchen, your favorite restaurants, your bedroom, your school and places where you like to hang out, like parks or recreation centers. Your map would also take in the roads and paths you use to move between these spots.

The size of each grizzly bear's home range depends on several things. One of the most important is food availability. The easier it is for a grizzly to find food, the smaller its home range. Grizzlies that live in coastal areas and eat salmon don't have to travel far to satisfy their hunger, so they have the smallest home ranges. Those that live farther inland, in the mountains or on the tundra or the prairies, usually have to search far and wide for their meals, so their home ranges are larger. Male grizzlies also generally have much larger home ranges than females in the same area.

When grizzlies grow up and become independent, they must find their own home range. Females usually settle within or close to their mother's home range. Males usually move farther away. JACOB W. FRANK/NPS/FLICKR.COM/ PUBLIC DOMAIN

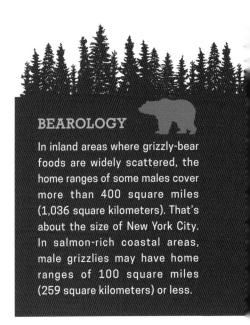

BEAROLOGY

In inland areas where grizzly-bear foods are widely scattered, the home ranges of some males cover more than 400 square miles (1,036 square kilometers). That's about the size of New York City. In salmon-rich coastal areas, male grizzlies may have home ranges of 100 square miles (259 square kilometers) or less.

A grizzly-bear family trudges through the snow in late fall. The cubs are almost as big as their mother, and the coming winter may be the last one they spend with her.
JOHN E. MARRIOTT, WILDERNESSPRINTS.COM

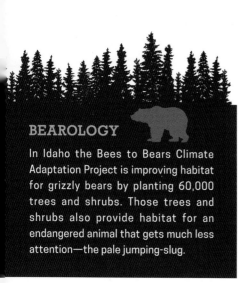

BEAROLOGY

In Idaho the Bees to Bears Climate Adaptation Project is improving habitat for grizzly bears by planting 60,000 trees and shrubs. Those trees and shrubs also provide habitat for an endangered animal that gets much less attention—the pale jumping-slug.

GUARDIANS OF THE WILDERNESS

All in all, grizzly bears do best in places with few people, few roads and little human activity. It's not that grizzlies can't live around people. They will tolerate us if they don't feel threatened. But many of us aren't comfortable having them nearby, so conflicts are common when we share space. People also often change the environment in ways that make it harder for grizzly bears to thrive. Each time we replace a berry field with a shopping mall or build a highway across a grizzly-bear route or pollute a river where they catch fish, we take away some of their habitat.

Large wilderness areas are particularly good places for grizzly bears. And grizzly bears can, in turn, help safeguard wilderness. That's because they are an *umbrella species*.

An umbrella species is an animal whose required habitat is so big that it stretches out over the habitats of many other animals and plants—like an umbrella. When we protect habitat for an umbrella species, members of its community also benefit.

Species that shelter under the grizzly bear's umbrella range from rare mosses to bull trout to wolverines. Some of those plants and animals also need their own special protections, but setting aside wilderness areas that are big enough for grizzlies is a good starting point for assisting them and the whole *ecosystem*.

Even though wilderness is important for grizzlies and grizzlies are important for wilderness, many of them now live in areas that have little or no true wilderness left. Those bears have no choice but to mix with humans. It's up to us to learn to coexist with grizzly bears to help them cope with the more crowded modern world.

Learning about Grizzlies in Classrooms without Walls

Allie Elluk-Housty is from Bella Bella, a small town on an island off the central coast of British Columbia. This whole area is Heiltsuk territory, where Allie's people have lived alongside grizzly bears for at least 14,000 years. Mostly they meet them on the mainland. Grizzlies rarely visit the island where Allie grew up, so she knew little about them until she started going to summer camp when she was 10.

Koeye Camp is on the mainland, about 30 miles (48 kilometers) south of Bella Bella. The campers get there by boat because there are no roads to Koeye. This wilderness camp is a place for Heiltsuk youth to celebrate their cultural traditions, study their language and learn about local plants and animals.

Allie went to Koeye as a camper for three years and worked there as a camp counselor for four more. Some summers, grizzlies appeared every few weeks. Others, they wandered through the camp or along the beach almost daily.

"It's a great place for a bear to live," Allie says. "If I were a bear, I would love to live there. There's lots of food. There's lots of land."

The campers learned to respect the grizzlies and safely share space with them. "We stayed out of their way as much as we could, because we're in their home," Allie explains. "They were there before us." Other safety practices included keeping the camp clean and free of garbage.

CAYCE FOSTER

Allie's grizzly-bear education continued when she worked on a study run by the Raincoast Conservation Foundation, the University of Victoria and the Heiltsuk Nation. The research involved collecting hair samples to identify and learn about individual bears. Allie was fascinated to discover how much information each tiny hair contains.

From seventh to eleventh grade Allie spent a few days each spring job-shadowing the biologists and working with them as a junior field technician. They traveled by boat or helicopter to remote field sites. At these locations the researchers had strung lines of barbed wire to snag hairs when bears walked by and brushed against it. Allie helped the crew remove the hair samples, label collection envelopes, fill out data sheets and prepare the sites for the next bears. From getting a taste of biology fieldwork to seeing bears to exploring new parts of her traditional territory, she loved it all.

> "I used to be scared of grizzly bears. Now they're my favorite animal on the earth."
> —Allie Elluk-Housty

Grizzly bears often rise on their hind legs when they are trying to identify something strange in their environment. Extra height gives them a better view. Even more important, it helps them pick up scents.
JOHN E. MARRIOTT, WILDERNESSPRINTS.COM

2
CHANGING VIEWS

IN THE BEGINNING

The grizzly bear's ancestors traveled from Asia to North America 50,000 to 100,000 years ago. Humans showed up much later. We can only guess how the bears felt about their new two-legged neighbors. But we know quite a bit about what grizzlies came to mean to Indigenous Peoples.

Every Indigenous group that knew grizzly bears developed a unique relationship with them, and these ancient ways live on today. From the Gwich'in to the Diné and from the Niitsitapi to the Yup'ik, each group has its own grizzly-bear stories, songs and dances. And each has specific beliefs, rituals and rules concerning grizzlies. But they all have one thing in common—deep respect for the grizzly bear. This respect is built on the understanding that people are part of nature, not separate from it or superior to other beings.

A grizzly bear in the northern Yukon sits on its haunches, surveying its surroundings.
JOHN E. MARRIOTT, WILDERNESSPRINTS.COM

BIG GRANDPA

It would take a whole book to describe all the different Indigenous traditions that relate to grizzlies, so I'll just tell you about a few. To learn more about Indigenous relationships with grizzly bears in your area, reach out to members of the Indigenous communities within whose territory you live.

North America's First Peoples learned how to minimize their risk of being harmed by grizzlies by paying attention to the bears' behavior and treating them courteously. Some Indigenous Peoples show respect for grizzlies by never saying their real name out loud or speaking about them directly. Instead they use a kind of code name or honorary title. For example, members of the Champagne and Aishihik First Nations in the Yukon traditionally use terms like "Our Brother" or "Big Grandpa" when they talk to or about grizzly bears.

A Kwakwaka'wakw grizzly-bear mask carved from red cedar, and claws made from whale-rib bones. Grizzly-Bear Dancers wear the mask and claws along with a bearskin or a wool blanket.
U'MISTA CULTURAL SOCIETY

Bear Dancer

Laura Grizzlypaws was born and raised in Lillooet, British Columbia, and belongs to the people of Xwisten, the St'át'imc Bear Clan. She lived with her grandparents until her grandmother died when Laura was five. After that she was separated from her family and placed in foster care, where she experienced abuse and neglect. During those dark years, Laura lost her sense of value and self-respect and struggled with her identity. She did poorly in school, became violent toward others and was repeatedly locked up in youth detention.

Then, at 17, she changed course. She sought out Elders and mentors in her community and asked them to teach her about St'át'imc culture and spirituality. "I had to find out who I was and am," she says. "All I ever wanted was to be St'át'imc, to be strong like my grandmother."

MAGGI WOO / COURTESY OF LAURA GRIZZLYPAWS

Since adopting this new way of life, Laura has achieved many things. She has learned to read and write the St'át'imc language and is contributing to preserving it. She has earned three university degrees. She has emerged as a talented singer-songwriter and hand drummer and won an Indigenous Music Award. And she has become an esteemed Bear Dancer and a spokesperson for the grizzly bear—Stálhalam.

The most important part of a traditional Grizzly-Bear Dancer's regalia is a grizzly-bear hide. Laura's came from a bear that was killed because it posed a threat to human safety. She named him Grizz and treats him with great care and respect, honoring his spirit. Still, she says, "it's more beautiful to see live grizzly bears than the one that I dance with."

When Laura pulls the heavy hide over her head and shoulders she is transformed. "I am one with the bear," she says. Dancing to the beat of a drum, she scoops her hands like a grizzly catching salmon. She shrugs her shoulders like a grizzly ambling along. She jumps and swats the air like a grizzly playfully trying to catch a butterfly or a bee.

The Bear Dance is known as a healing dance, a celebration dance and even an inspirational dance. When there is cultural work to do, only certain people, like Laura, may dance the Bear Dance. But at community events, everyone is welcome to join in—adults and children alike.

"The grizzly bear is held in the highest respect in our culture," Laura says. But the number of grizzlies living within St'át'imc territory has been declining ever since settlers arrived. They are now among the most endangered grizzly bears in Canada. The St'át'imc and neighboring First Nations are working hard to ensure their survival.

"If we look after the grizzly bear, then we're looking after the land itself and all the things that need the land to survive."

—Laura Grizzlypaws

Wearers of this Pawnee bear-claw necklace were protected in war and against sickness by the power of the bear. It took many grizzlies to make it, since only the middle three claws from the front paws were used. Pawnee Bear Doctors Society, Nebraska, Bear Claw Necklace, before 1870, remade 1920s. Native Arts acquisition fund in honor of Norman Feder, 1973.247. PHOTOGRAPH © DENVER ART MUSEUM

General George Armstrong Custer (center) poses with a grizzly bear he killed in South Dakota in 1874. The hunting party included Custer's favorite scout, Bloody Knife (on the left), and Colonel William Ludlow and Private John Noonan (on the right). COURTESY OF THE NATIONAL PARK SERVICE, LITTLE BIGHORN BATTLEFIELD NATIONAL MONUMENT

Many Indigenous Peoples recognize a close bond between themselves and their bear neighbors, whether they are grizzlies, black bears or polar bears. One expression of this belief comes from the Yavapai, who live in Arizona. Their culture says that bears are like people except they can't make fire.

In British Columbia, the St'át'imc honor the grizzly bear as a teacher. They speak of how the grizzly bear shared important life skills with their ancestors, such as where and when they should go to gather berries, dig for roots and fish for salmon. That's why their traditional diet is similar to the diet of grizzlies living in their territory. St'át'imc stories also explain that the grizzly bear taught women how to be mothers and gave them the gift of being able to have twins. Because of their special relationship with grizzlies, the St'át'imc do not hunt them or eat their meat.

RULES OF THE HUNT

Some other Indigenous cultures have a tradition of hunting grizzly bears, which provide meat for food, fur for warmth and fat for cooking and for medicine. Today Indigenous people who hunt grizzly bears usually use guns. In the past they had to get close enough to kill the bears with spears, arrows or clubs. Sometimes they caught their quarry first. For example, a Champagne and Aishihik hunter might have made a snare out of a loop of dried moosehide or built a trap from heavy logs.

Each Indigenous community that allows grizzly-bear hunting has traditional teachings that guide this activity. They cover things like how and when to hunt and how to show respect for both live and dead bears.

A grizzly-bear mother and cub walk past the Koeye Bighouse. The Heiltsuk erected this building on the site of one of their ancestral villages as a place to practice and teach their culture and language. The Heiltsuk call these bears *Náṇ*.
KYLE ARTELLE

The Iñupiat of northwest Alaska teach that bears have excellent hearing, so bear hunters should not talk about their hunting plans, brag about how many bears they have killed, speak negatively about bears or make fun of them. After Iñupiaq hunters kill a grizzly bear, the first thing they must do is remove the small tongue-bone and carefully dispose of it. This ritual ensures that the bear's spirit has gone elsewhere and safeguards the hunter. Once hunters have butchered a bear, they share the meat and fat with their whole community. Traditionally Iñupiaq women and girls were not allowed to eat bear meat, but nowadays they are. The bear's hide is usually given to the person who killed it or to the oldest hunter in the group.

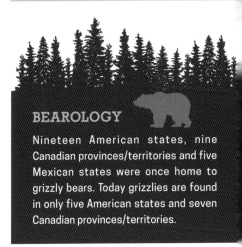

BEAROLOGY

Nineteen American states, nine Canadian provinces/territories and five Mexican states were once home to grizzly bears. Today grizzlies are found in only five American states and seven Canadian provinces/territories.

BEAROLOGY

Enos Mills was an American naturalist, conservationist and author. He spent 30 years observing grizzly bears, mostly in Colorado. In 1919 he published a book about his experiences called *The Grizzly: Our Greatest Wild Animal*. It helped change public attitudes toward grizzlies and build support for protecting them.

ERYNMILLS/WIKIMEDIA COMMONS/CC BY-SA 4.0

STRANGER DANGER

When Europeans arrived in the late 1400s, North America had about 100,000 grizzly bears. But as the newcomers moved westward across the continent, grizzly-bear numbers fell rapidly. Many European explorers and settlers were terrified of grizzlies and believed the only way to stay safe was to gun down every one they met. Some just enjoyed the challenge of hunting such a formidable foe. Thousands of grizzly bears were also killed for their hides, which were sold to fur traders for large sums. Countless others were shot, trapped or poisoned to protect cattle and sheep. Even grizzlies that never set foot on a farm or ranch were considered fair game by landowners, bounty hunters and government agents.

As time went on it became harder and harder for the remaining bears to find suitable places to live. More people on the land meant fewer large areas where grizzlies could go about their business undisturbed. In some cases it also meant less food.

Grizzly bears living on the prairies faced the worst food crisis. The massive herds of bison that roamed the Great Plains had always been their main source of protein. But a slaughter led by European settlers reduced the number of bison from around 30 million to about 1,000. Many of the hungry bears figured cows were a good substitute for bison, but the ranchers had no tolerance for the cattle killers.

By 1900 grizzly bears had been eradicated from Minnesota, North and South Dakota, Nebraska, Kansas, Oklahoma and Texas. They vanished from Saskatchewan, Manitoba, New Mexico, California, Utah, Arizona and Oregon in the 1920s and 1930s, and from the Ungava region of northern Quebec and Labrador in the late 1940s. Mexico lost its last grizzly bear in 1976, in the state of Sonora.

A grizzly bear feeds on a bison carcass in the Yellowstone River. Bison were once a key food for grizzlies living on the Great Plains. Yellowstone National Park is one of the few places where this predator-prey relationship still exists.
JIM PEACO/YELLOWSTONE NATIONAL PARK/ FLICKR.COM/PUBLIC DOMAIN

California's last wild grizzly bear was killed in 1922. In 1953 the grizzly bear was chosen as California's official state animal. The state flag featuring the grizzly was adopted in 1911 and still flies today.
WILLIAM SHERMAN/GETTY IMAGES

Feeding grizzlies and black bears was a popular tourist activity in Yellowstone National Park until the 1970s. Cubs quickly learned that treats could be found if they approached people sitting in their cars.
CHIPPIX/SHUTTERSTOCK.COM

Colorado's last one was shot in 1979. What makes this record even sadder is that we know exactly when and where the last grizzlies in many of these places died and who fired the guns that killed them.

THE TURNING POINT

As the 20th century unfolded, grizzly-bear numbers kept falling, especially in southern Canada and the Lower 48 states. By 1975 only about 700 to 800 grizzlies remained south of the Canada-United States border. Many people feared that these bears too would be wiped out. At that point the government of the United States decided to take strong action. The grizzly bears of the Lower 48 states were declared a threatened species and given protection under the country's new Endangered Species Act.

A wildlife veterinarian and biologists prepare a young grizzly bear for its return to the wild after a stay at the Northern Lights Wildlife Shelter. The orange wrap protects its eyes while it is tranquilized. They have fitted the bear with a GPS collar so they can track it after it is released.
JOHN E. MARRIOTT, WILDERNESSPRINTS.COM

Even though the Threatened Species label didn't apply to grizzly bears in Alaska and Canada, it was a big step toward a new relationship between grizzlies and people everywhere. Another big step was taken in 1991. That was the year the Committee on the Status of Endangered Wildlife in Canada gave Canadian grizzly bears Special Concern status.

Bears with GPS collars aren't stuck with them forever. The collars are made to fall off within a few years—or sooner if put on a young bear with a growing neck. Biologists can also send a satellite signal to unfasten them.
JOHN E. MARRIOTT, WILDERNESSPRINTS.COM

Since 1975 grizzly-bear numbers have increased in some places and decreased in others. The greatest gains have been in the Greater Yellowstone Ecosystem. This area covers roughly 34,000 square miles (88,060 square kilometers) of Idaho, Montana and Wyoming, including Yellowstone National Park, Grand Teton National Park and other public lands. In 1975 only about 136 grizzlies remained in the Greater Yellowstone Ecosystem. There are now about 1,000, thanks to the protection they have received.

Biologists try to keep track of how many grizzly bears are in each state, province and territory, but generally they can only estimate their numbers. It's difficult and expensive to get exact numbers because most grizzlies live in areas that are hard to reach and work in. Counting grizzlies is also challenging because they are widely scattered across the landscape. Here are the current *population* estimates:

ALASKA—25,000 to 39,000

BRITISH COLUMBIA—15,000

YUKON—6,000

NORTHWEST TERRITORIES—4,000

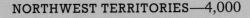

WYOMING, MONTANA, IDAHO AND WASHINGTON combined—at least 1,900

NUNAVUT—1,500

ALBERTA—900

NORTHERN MANITOBA—a few

From Fear to Fascination

Clayton Lamb met his first wild grizzly bear when he was 10 years old. "I thought I was going to die," he recalls.

Clayton and his dad were hunting deer in southern British Columbia when they spotted a big bear with silvery fur about 330 yards (300 meters) away in a long narrow clear-cut. They immediately called out to let the bear know they were around. But instead of retreating, it turned and began walking toward them. Time to head for their truck! Unfortunately, they would have to pass the approaching bear to get there.

The next heart-pounding 10 minutes felt like an eternity. As father and son edged along one side of the clear-cut, the grizzly sauntered along the other. Clayton's fear increased every time the bear slipped out of sight. Things got even scarier when they passed each other, heading in opposite directions. By then they were less than 33 yards (30 meters) apart.

LAURA SMIT

The moment they reached the truck, Clayton burst into tears. Only later did he realize the bear wasn't out to get them. They were just in his way.

Fifteen years after that encounter, Clayton found himself back in nearly the same place. This time he was there as a biologist doing research, the first of many grizzly-bear studies he has worked on since then.

JANET NG

Some of Clayton's research begins with collecting hair samples from snag sites. To set up a hair-snag site, he douses a pile of branches with a blend of rotten cow's blood and fish oil that smells awful to humans but enticing to bears. Then he surrounds the pile with a single strand of barbed wire. Curious bears duck under the wire to investigate and painlessly leave behind tufts of fur.

Clayton sends the hairs to a lab for *DNA* analysis. From genetic information in each sample he learns the identity and sex of the bear it came from. He also learns how different bears are related to one another.

Clayton also does research that involves capturing grizzly bears and temporarily putting them to sleep with drugs. While a bear is asleep, Clayton and his crew weigh it, measure its body fat and pluck a few hairs. They also fit it with a *GPS* collar that the bear will wear for the next few years.

The collar transmits location data to a satellite, and the satellite sends it to Clayton's computer. He uses the data to map the bear's travels and learn about its activities. If a collared grizzly bear dies, the GPS leads him to its body so he can figure out the cause of death.

Clayton says his least favorite part of the work is handling the disgusting concoction he uses to attract grizzlies to snag sites. The best part is getting to spend his summers eating huckleberries and learning about bears.

"We were where the bear wanted to go, farther back into the wild. And he was where we wanted to go, closer to our truck."

—Clayton Lamb

This little cub looks like it's waving hello. Actually the photographer caught it in mid-tumble as it flung one leg into the air.
KEN CONGER/NPS PHOTO

TEDDY BEAR OR TERROR?

When you hear the words *grizzly bear*, what picture pops into your mind? Maybe it's a funny cartoon figure like Grizz from *We Bare Bears* or Yogi Bear. Or maybe it's a ferocious beast that would eat you in the blink of an eye. We all know that cartoon bears aren't real, but many people don't realize that memes of menacing grizzlies are just as misleading.

Being afraid of getting hurt or killed by a grizzly bear is understandable. After all, they are large, powerful animals with sharp teeth and claws. But the truth is, they hardly ever use their strength against humans. Grizzlies are remarkably patient with people and just as keen to avoid confrontations as we are.

Grizzlies only roar when they're feeling highly stressed or argumentative. More subtle signs of grizzly-bear stress include yawning or stiffening their posture. Huffing and moaning are intermediate mood indicators.
SCOTT E. READ/SHUTTERSTOCK.COM

Mother grizzly bears are extremely protective of their cubs, especially when they are less than a year old, like this trio. SERGEY URYADNIKOV/SHUTTERSTOCK.COM

When grizzlies do harm people, it's almost always because they are defending their cubs or their food or their own personal space, particularly when they have been taken by surprise. When grizzly bears become aware of nearby humans, generally their first choice of action is to quietly slip away. If they don't have time to retreat and they feel threatened, they may react defensively. They might make sounds or use body language to signal their discomfort, but they don't usually charge or attack. Most close encounters between people and grizzly bears end without any direct contact.

To get an idea of how extremely uncommon grizzly-bear attacks are, we can look at statistics from Yellowstone National Park. Yellowstone has lots of grizzlies and lots of human visitors. But the odds of any of those visitors being injured by a grizzly bear are one in 2.7 million.

A grizzly-bear family bolts across the highway in Jasper National Park. Slippery, wet snow adds to the danger for the bears and for approaching cars.
JOHN E. MARRIOTT, WILDERNESSPRINTS.COM

Fatal attacks are even rarer. Since Yellowstone opened in 1872, only seven or eight people have been killed by grizzly bears in the park. (We don't know the exact number because one of those people was killed by an unidentified bear.) Falling trees also killed seven people in Yellowstone during the same period. All of those deaths were tragic, but it's easier to prevent getting on a grizzly bear's bad side than to predict when a tree will topple.

TROUBLESOME HUMANS

Far more grizzly bears are killed by humans every year than the other way around. Many die after being struck by trains, trucks or cars. But accidents aren't the only cause of death. Licensed hunters can legally kill grizzly bears in Alaska and parts of Canada. Grizzlies are also sometimes killed by hunters who pursue them illegally or mistake them for black bears. And occasionally people kill grizzlies when they fear for their own lives. Even the people whose job is looking after grizzly bears sometimes end up killing them. In places where people and grizzlies are neighbors, wildlife managers too often have to *euthanize* bears that have developed dangerous habits, usually because of human behavior.

The never-ending search for food can push grizzlies into parking lots and other poor habitats.
STEVE BOICE/SHUTTERSTOCK.COM

Humans also harm grizzly bears indirectly. Damaging or destroying their habitat makes their lives harder and more stressful, especially if it reduces their food supply. Loss of habitat affects individual grizzlies. It also affects the whole population, since underfed bears have fewer cubs and shorter lives than well-fed bears.

Despite these challenges, there is plenty of hope for this species. Many people are striving to help grizzlies recover from past harms and shield them from current and future threats. Those efforts all start with understanding grizzly-bear life.

Grizzlies look half human when they stand on their hind legs. That may be one reason why many people feel a strong bond with these bears.

JOHN E. MARRIOTT, WILDERNESSPRINTS.COM

3
IT'S A BEAR'S LIFE

CIRCLING THE SEASONS

Grizzly bears have long lives compared to many other mammals. In the wild they typically live about 20 to 25 years. Some keep going well into their 30s. Throughout their lives grizzlies follow the same seasonal cycle every year. They snooze through winter and spend spring, summer and fall fattening up before crawling back into bed.

WINTER DREAMS

The grizzly bear's winter slumber is called *hibernation*. During hibernation a grizzly bear's heart rate slows to just a few beats a minute, and its body temperature drops slightly. Sometimes the bear stretches or adjusts its position, and it will wake up if disturbed.

Grizzly bears hibernate in order to conserve energy during winter, when food is scarce. They don't eat or drink at all while in their dens.

BEAROLOGY

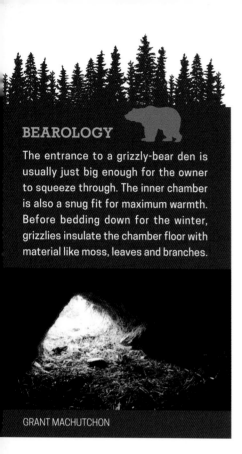

The entrance to a grizzly-bear den is usually just big enough for the owner to squeeze through. The inner chamber is also a snug fit for maximum warmth. Before bedding down for the winter, grizzlies insulate the chamber floor with material like moss, leaves and branches.

GRANT MACHUTCHON

Grizzly bears usually dig a new den each year. It's a big job that can take several days and involve moving up to a ton of dirt.
EMILY MESNER/NPS PHOTO

That's usually about four to six months! How long a bear hibernates depends partly on the weather. In the coldest, snowiest parts of Alaska and northern Canada, some grizzlies hibernate for more than half the year.

Female grizzly bears that are pregnant or caring for cubs hibernate the longest. They typically enter their dens around mid-November and stay put until late April or early May. Adult males have the shortest hibernation periods. They might not tuck in until December and may emerge as early as March.

Grizzly bears survive this long period of fasting by drawing on energy stored in their fat and muscle. Amazingly, they can do this without needing to defecate or urinate the whole time they are hibernating.

A suitable den site is key to a good winter's sleep. Grizzlies often climb high up mountainsides to make their dens. They find it easiest to dig on steep slopes, and they like places where there will be plenty of snow for insulation. Sometimes they tunnel under tree roots or boulders for extra security.

When grizzly bears want to sleep or rest at other times of year, they dig shallow pits in the ground. These are often called day beds but may be used during the day or at night.

Researchers measure a day bed tucked between two logs at the base of a tree. Grizzlies look for bed sites like this, which provide some cover and shelter.
JACOB W. FRANK/NPS PHOTO

THE FIRST YEAR

Grizzly-bear cubs are born while their mothers are hibernating, usually in late January or early February. They weigh little more than a pound (453 grams) at birth, have no fur and are about the size of a soda can. Their eyes don't open until they are about three weeks old. For their first three or four months, the sleepy cubs stay snuggled up to their mother, drinking the rich milk she provides. By the time they leave the den, they weigh 10 to 20 pounds (4.5 to 9 kilograms).

Grizzly bears usually have one, two or three cubs. Occasionally there are four in a litter. Mothers raise the cubs on their own. It's a big job that includes protecting them, making sure they get lots to eat and educating them

Young grizzly-bear cubs nursing. Their mother's milk will provide important nourishment for them throughout their first summer as they gradually add other foods to their diet.
EMILY MESNER/NPS PHOTO

Two bright-eyed youngsters explore the world on an early June morning, not long after leaving the den where they were born.
JOHN E. MARRIOTT, WILDERNESSPRINTS.COM

about the world. The youngsters stay with their mother for two to three years, growing and gaining survival skills. Cubs learn by closely watching everything their mother does and copying her actions. As they travel around they are constantly adding to their mental map of important places, especially where to find different types of food.

During their first summer they continue nursing but also start to eat adult foods. When it's time to return to the den, a healthy first-year cub will be about 10 times heavier than when it emerged in the spring.

But many cubs don't survive that long. One risk they face is that adult male grizzly bears sometimes try to kill them. The reason for these deadly attacks is that a female

At about four months old, this cub is inexperienced and defenseless. For now it is completely dependent on its mother for guidance and protection.
JOHN E. MARRIOTT, WILDERNESSPRINTS.COM

grizzly can only raise one litter at a time and will not mate while she is caring for them. If a male gets rid of a female bear's cubs, he can mate with her sooner than if he waits for them to grow up and go off on their own. Biologists aren't sure how often males kill cubs. But they do know that mother grizzly bears try to keep their families well away from males. They are also fiercely protective of their cubs, whether the threat is another grizzly bear or a human.

GOING SOLO

Young grizzlies leave their mothers during their third or fourth spring. At this point they are like teenagers who have a few more years to go before they become full-grown adults. Biologists call them subadults. For safety and companionship, subadult siblings sometimes stick together for a while. They may even share a den during their first winter away from their mother.

Once they become adults, male grizzly bears are mostly loners. The only time they purposely seek out other grizzlies is when they're looking for mates in late spring or early summer. To get close to females, they often have to compete with other males. These contests involve lots of showmanship but little actual fighting. Most males don't win the chance to mate until they are five to ten years old.

Subadult females are also quite solitary. That changes around age five to eight, when they are ready to become mothers. After that they spend most of their lives raising their young. Now and then two families of mothers and cubs will hang out for a while during spring or summer—a bit like having playdates.

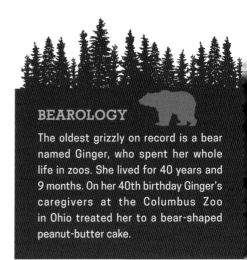

BEAROLOGY

The oldest grizzly on record is a bear named Ginger, who spent her whole life in zoos. She lived for 40 years and 9 months. On her 40th birthday Ginger's caregivers at the Columbus Zoo in Ohio treated her to a bear-shaped peanut-butter cake.

Play-fighting with siblings helps young grizzlies prepare for adulthood. As they wrestle they build their strength and improve their physical abilities.
JOHN E. MARRIOTT, WILDERNESSPRINTS.COM

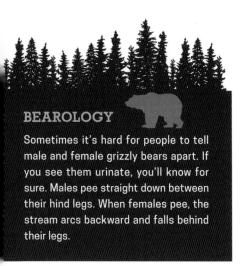

BEAROLOGY

Sometimes it's hard for people to tell male and female grizzly bears apart. If you see them urinate, you'll know for sure. Males pee straight down between their hind legs. When females pee, the stream arcs backward and falls behind their legs.

Two grizzly bears struggle to gain possession of a salmon. Contact combat like this is uncommon. In conflict situations the less dominant bear usually backs down and retreats rather than risk getting hurt.
DAI MAR TAMARACK/SHUTTERSTOCK.COM

Grizzly bears will also come together when there's a large amount of food available in one place. A river swarming with salmon or a big berry field full of ripe fruit is more than one bear can defend. It's also more than one bear can eat, so it's a waste of energy to try to keep others away. The richer the feast, the more tolerant of company grizzly bears are. But they still sometimes quarrel over the best feeding spots. Adult males always rule in these situations. Adult females and subadults of both sexes will quickly retreat if one of the big bosses warns them off.

GETTING THE MESSAGE ACROSS

Grizzly bears use sounds and body language for close-range communication. They need to be good at communicating when they come across each other so they can avoid fighting with their teeth and claws. There's too great a risk of being injured or killed in a brawl. Good communication skills are equally important within families.

Mothers speak to their cubs with grunts and moans to warn them of dangers and give them instructions. And cubs bawl if they lose contact with their mothers.

Grizzly bears that feel threatened or stressed by the presence of another grizzly or a person express their feelings with huffs, woofs, snorts, growls or roars. Sometimes they make popping sounds with their jaws or clack their teeth.

Agitated grizzly bears also rely on facial expressions, gestures and movements to get their message across. The position of their ears, mouth, head and whole body sends important signals to any nearby bear. That bear will respond with its own body language. For example, if you are a subadult grizzly and an older male approaches you with a direct stare and a stiff-legged walk, he's telling you to get lost. The smart response is to turn your head to one side to avoid meeting his gaze and back away—basically saying, "Hey, dude, no worries. I'm out of here."

Two female grizzlies—both with cubs nearby—argue over a prime fishing spot. Confronting an opponent with an open mouth is a kind of bear body language called *jawing*. It sends a "back off" message that usually keeps squabbles from becoming violent.
JOHN E. MARRIOTT, WILDERNESSPRINTS.COM

A grizzly-bear mother and cub communicate silently as they gently touch noses.
KENT MILLER/NPS PHOTO

THE NOSE KNOWS

Grizzly bears can also communicate with each other when they are far apart. They do this by rubbing against tree trunks or similar objects, such as power poles or fence posts. As they rub, they leave scent messages for other bears to find.

The scents come from special sweat glands in their skin. Grizzlies use various techniques to spread them around. Often they stand on their back legs and rub their backs or chests against the tree. Other times they stand on all four legs or sit or lie down as they rub their sides, rumps, heads or feet. They may also scratch or bite the trunk.

A subadult grizzly hugs a large pine tree as it rubs its chest against the rough bark, leaving a scent message for other members of its community.
JOHN E. MARRIOTT, WILDERNESSPRINTS.COM

Grizzly-bear rub trees are like community notice boards where anyone can post announcements. They are always located in places where other bears are likely to pass by and sniff out the messages, such as along popular travel routes. Grizzlies return to favorite rub trees year after year. Over time the bark becomes smooth and shiny or gouged and scarred. Hairs often get caught in crevices or stuck in the sap that oozes from the scratches and bite marks.

Sometimes there is a line of shallow oval depressions leading up to a rub tree. This is called a stomp trail. Bears—usually males—make the depressions by grinding their feet into the ground as they approach the tree, leaving their scent as they go. Each bear that stomps up the path places its paws in the same spots, making the footprints more obvious.

We can't directly decipher grizzly-bear scent messages, but biologists believe they give other grizzlies important information about who left them and how recently they were there.

HUNGRY AS A BEAR

Grizzly bears are omnivores. That means they eat both plants and animals. Unless you are a vegetarian or a vegan, you're an omnivore too. But you are probably a pickier eater than a grizzly bear. Grizzlies eat an incredible variety of foods and have many ways of filling their bellies. They hunt, fish, *scavenge*, dig, pluck, munch and more.

No other North American mammal is known to eat as many different foods as the grizzly bear. The full list includes hundreds of items, though which ones a particular bear eats depends on what is available and most nutritious. Animals are important sources of protein and fat for all grizzlies, but they can be hard to come by. In many areas, plants make up 80 to 90 percent of the grizzly-bear diet.

A grizzly bear rubs its back against a rub tree, unaware of the motion-activated trail camera that is taking its picture. Trail cameras let biologists study the action around rub trees without disturbing the bears.
MELANIE CLAPHAM

A stomp trail in the Khutzeymateen/K'tzim-a-deen Grizzly Bear Sanctuary. This line of deep footprints in the mossy forest floor is the work of many grizzly bears, treading the same path over many years.
FRANCES BACKHOUSE

A large male grizzly bear takes advantage of low tide to dig for clams in mud flats on the north coast of British Columbia.
JOHN E. MARRIOTT, WILDERNESSPRINTS.COM

No matter what's on the grocery list, eating is a full-time job for grizzly bears. They lose 15 to 30 percent of their body weight during hibernation and spend the rest of the year working to get that weight back. When they're not hibernating, grizzlies devote most of their waking hours to looking for food and eating. Springtime rations can be skimpy, so they often keep losing fat until late spring or early summer. Then they start to bulk up again.

As soon as grizzlies come out of their dens, they head for places where the snow has melted away and plants are beginning to sprout. Sunny slopes and valley bottoms are prime springtime feeding locations. From there they move on to other favorite feeding sites, following a course set by their stomachs.

Diet Detective

Grizzlies will eat almost anything. Just ask wildlife biologist Jennifer Fortin-Noreus. Over the years she has examined a lot of grizzly-bear poop—or *scat*, as scientists call it—and found many different things in it. Some of the strangest remains she has come across in grizzly-bear scat are frogs and ducklings.

Jennifer now works with the US Fish and Wildlife Service's Grizzly Bear Recovery Program in Montana, but she began studying grizzlies in Alaska on the Kenai National Wildlife Refuge. She soon learned that scat from bears that have been eating salmon smells much worse than scat full of berries. She scooped plenty of poop, stinky or not, and later picked it apart to see what it contained. She identified berries from their seeds, other plants from bits of leaves, and salmon from bones and scales.

JOY ERLENBANBACH

Jennifer also collected samples of the foods the grizzly bears were eating. Measuring how much protein, fat and energy was in each type of food helped her figure out how grizzlies pack on the pounds.

Bear hairs plucked from barbed-wire snag sites offered more clues. Jennifer sent them to a special lab where two chemical elements were analyzed. The nitrogen in these hairs showed the proportion of plants and animals in each bear's diet. Sulfur revealed whether the plants and animals a bear had eaten had come from the land or had once lived in the ocean, like salmon.

All this evidence helped Jennifer understand how these coastal grizzly bears choose their meals in fall. "Salmon has the highest protein content, so you would think they would just eat salmon all day long," she says. But they don't. Now and then they go and fill up on berries instead. That's not because they're bored with fish. It's because berries are high in fattening carbohydrates. The bears need both salmon and berries to get the right balance of protein and carbohydrates when preparing for hibernation.

Jennifer has also done diet detective work in Yellowstone National Park. Her research there confirmed that grizzly bears are very good at making the most of whatever food they can find and are always trying new things.

> "Grizzly bears are very large and have to spend a lot of time eating. We need to give them the space to do that safely."
>
> —Jennifer Fortin-Noreus

Borry scat
ROB RICH

Scat containing whitebark-pine seeds
JACOB W. FRANK/NPS/FLICKR.COM/
PUBLIC DOMAIN

Grizzly-bear hair
CLAYTON LAMB

It's mid-October, and this grizzly bear in Denali National Park will soon be hibernating. For now it's eating as much as it can to fatten up for the long Alaska winter. NPS PHOTO

EXTREME EATING

In late summer grizzly bears start bingeing on high-energy foods like berries and salmon, and they don't quit until they are ready to hibernate. This is called *hyperphagia*, a fancy way of saying "extreme eating." During hyperphagia grizzlies feed for up to 20 hours every day and gain as much as 3.6 pounds (1.6 kilograms) a day. Successful salmon eaters can consume 30,000 calories or more daily. That's like you eating 50 or more cheeseburgers in one day!

The point of this gluttony is to store enough fuel to get through a winter of no eating and the lean times in early spring. A thick layer of fat also provides good insulation against the cold during hibernation. Female grizzly bears need extra stored energy so they can give birth and produce milk while hibernating.

BELLIES FULL OF BERRIES

Grizzly bears love all kinds of berries and are expert pickers. When they're on a roll, they can scarf down thousands of berries in an hour. Their ability to see color helps them spot the ripe fruit. They use their nimble paws, lips and tongues to harvest it. If the berries aren't at head level, grizzlies stand on their hind legs to reach them or bend down the branches with their front paws.

Grizzlies also eat other parts of many different plants, including leaves, flowers and roots. They favor newly sprouted greenery in spring because it is easiest to digest. When digging for roots, they prefer the ones that are thick and starchy, similar to carrots.

Whitebark-pine seeds are a specialty food for grizzly bears in some parts of the Rockies and other mountain ranges. These tasty morsels are about the size of corn kernels and full of fat, protein and carbohydrates. Every two to four years, whitebark pines produce loads of seed-filled cones. Red squirrels harvest the cones from the treetops and bury big batches of them for later use. But grizzlies sometimes spoil their plans. When a bear's nose leads it to one of these stashes, it will happily polish off the whole lot while the owner complains in vain from the branches above.

A grizzly bear plucks soapberries—also known as buffaloberries—from a bush. To humans these berries taste bitter and soapy, but they are a major part of the grizzly-bear diet in dry inland habitats throughout western North America.
KEN CONGER/NPS PHOTO

Grizzly bears eat a lot of greens in spring and early summer while waiting for other foods to come into season.
KENT MILLER/NPS PHOTO

A grizzly hunches over the body of an animal it has killed. The bear will guard its prize fiercely until it has eaten its fill. That may take several days.
GREY MOUNTAIN PHOTO/SHUTTERSTOCK.COM

Freshly churned-up ground in this mountain meadow shows where a grizzly bear was digging for plant roots. A hunt for burrowing animals generally leaves behind deeper holes.
CLAYTON LAMB

FROM BISON TO BUGS

With their muscular shoulders and front legs, flexible paws and long, sharp claws, grizzly bears are well-equipped for all kinds of hunting. They prey on many other animals, but no other animals except humans kill them for food. That makes the grizzly bear an *apex predator*, which means it is at the top of the food chain.

• The largest animals grizzly bears ever kill are grazers, including bison, caribou, elk, moose, deer and mountain goats. Mostly they target the calves, which have no horns or antlers to defend themselves with and can't run as fast as adults. But a big male grizzly bear can bring down a full-grown bison.

• Grizzlies are very good at digging ground squirrels, marmots and pocket gophers out of their underground burrows. A bear can move huge amounts of earth as it plows its way through a ground-squirrel colony, gulping down its victims as it goes.

- Grizzly bears also eat *invertebrates*. They overturn logs, rip into rotting stumps and dig up fields to find ants, earthworms and grubs. In coastal habitats they often dig for clams in the mud at low tide. They also pry mussels and barnacles off rocks and flip loose stones to get at crabs and other small creatures hiding beneath them.

- Army cutworm moths are another grizzly-bear delicacy. Every summer swarms of these insects fly from the Great Plains to places high in the Rocky Mountains. They spend their nights in *alpine* meadows filled with wildflowers, tanking up on sweet nectar. During the day they sleep in dense clusters under boulders on steep, rocky slopes. Grizzlies roll the rocks over to expose the moths and lick them up by the dozens with their long, flexible tongues. Each moth is as fatty as a nugget of butter, and a grizzly bear can consume up to 40,000 of them in a day.

A grizzly bear paws through gravel and stones, searching for invertebrates that may be hiding beneath them.
MARY LEWANDOWSKI/NPS PHOTO

A grizzly bear's front claws measure 2 to 4 inches (5 to 10 centimeters) long and are excellent digging tools.
DENNIS W. DONOHUE/SHUTTERSTOCK.COM

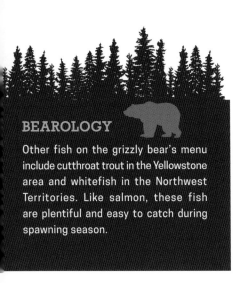

BEAROLOGY

Other fish on the grizzly bear's menu include cutthroat trout in the Yellowstone area and whitefish in the Northwest Territories. Like salmon, these fish are plentiful and easy to catch during spawning season.

Salmon traveling upriver to spawn have to leap high in places to get past the water pouring over tall rocks. If they are unlucky, a waiting grizzly bear will grab them in midair.
ROBERT FRASHURE/SHUTTERSTOCK.COM

SENSATIONAL SALMON

Every year millions of salmon leave the Pacific Ocean and head up rivers and streams to the places where they will breed for their first and only time and then die. When they reach their destination, the females deposit their eggs in the streambed gravel, and the males fertilize them. This is called *spawning*.

Some salmon travel only a short distance from the coast before they spawn. Others swim as far inland as the Yukon, the middle of British Columbia or central Idaho. Grizzlies that live along these routes devour enormous quantities of salmon and depend less on plant foods than grizzlies in other areas do. Thanks to their nutritious fishy diet, the salmon eaters are much bigger than their inland relatives and usually have larger litters.

Areas of shallow, fast-flowing water give grizzlies the best fishing opportunities. Dominant males claim those spots first. Other bears fish wherever they can. The way grizzlies catch salmon depends on the situation. Common strategies include leaping from a *logjam*, charging into the water from shore and standing motionless in midstream, waiting for salmon to swim by.

A grizzly bear charges into the river, intent on seizing a salmon it has spotted from the shore.
PAUL SOUDERS/GETTY IMAGES

Grizzlies usually pin their prey to the bottom with one or both of their front feet or grab it with their teeth. Occasionally they swat a fish right out of the water. After salmon have spawned, they become weaker and easier to catch.

When there is an abundance of salmon, grizzly bears often just eat the fatty eggs, brain and skin. But they become less fussy as spawning season winds down. Finally, when there are no more live salmon, they dig into any dead carcasses that are still around.

LEFTOVERS—YUM!

Grizzly bears don't mind eating leftovers, even when they are half rotten. They'll go for any easy meal. In fact, grizzlies that aren't salmon eaters get most of their meat from animals that were already dead before the bears showed up. In early spring they scavenge the remains of large animals like bison or caribou that died over the winter and were buried by snow. They will also steal freshly killed prey from wolves any time they can. They might have to fight for the prize, but driving off a few wolves is no problem for a determined grizzly bear.

Not Your Average High School Job

One day when Bryce Hennings was in high school in Hinton, Alberta, he heard that a local organization called fRI Research was looking for students to work on a grizzly-bear study. Bryce and his friend Adam Danis jumped at the opportunity. They were both hired, along with two other twelfth graders, Morgan Bailey and Hunter Sewid.

The study was focused on a quarry in the Rocky Mountains near Hinton, where limestone is mined to make cement. The quarry managers wanted to know how grizzlies were using the area so they could do a better job of sharing the landscape with them.

From left to right: Student researchers Bryce, Adam, Hunter and Morgan, and biologist Anja Sorensen.
KAREN GRAHAM

When the four students and three project biologists began their fieldwork in early April, the steep slopes around the quarry were still buried in snow. "It was pretty cold when we first got out there," Bryce recalls. But they were soon sweating as they waded through the knee-high drifts to reach their first sampling site.

After digging out an area the size of a large driveway, they gathered branches and piled them on the ground. Then they drenched the pile with a liquid scent lure that smelled like a dead animal and corralled it with a strand of barbed wire. They also mounted a motion-activated *trail camera* on a tree to record pictures of the bears they hoped to attract.

In early May they set up two more sampling sites. A few weeks later they got their first results. The trail-camera images showed a grizzly rolling around on the branches at one site. There were also a few bear hairs caught in the barbed wire. Bryce and his friends could hardly wait for their next visit.

Over the next couple of months the crew returned every second weekend to gather snagged bear hairs, add scent lure to the branch piles and download pictures from the cameras. The job ended in June, but there was more excitement to come. That fall the study won the North American round of an international competition for projects that boost *biodiversity* at cement quarries. Each student received a share of the prize money, along with the satisfaction of having contributed to grizzly-bear science. "It was good to feel like what we did mattered," Bryce says.

> "For me, the highlight was the firsthand experience with field research. I would definitely recommend it to anyone who is interested in going into the science field."
>
> —Bryce Hennings

COMMUNITY HELPERS

As grizzly bears feed themselves, they also feed some of their neighbors and increase ecosystem health. One way that salmon-eating grizzlies do this is by serving up free meals to other fish lovers. The bears usually carry their catch to shore before they start eating. Once they have taken what they want, scavengers such as ravens, gulls, otters and minks move in.

The massive amounts of salmon that grizzly bears haul out of the water also feed streamside forests. Salmon are loaded with nitrogen, which is an essential plant food. Grizzly bears spread this valuable fertilizer by scattering carcasses and pooping all along salmon-spawning rivers and streams.

Their berry eating provides different kinds of community benefits. Grizzlies can't digest berry seeds, so they come out the other end unharmed. For deer mice, red-backed voles and other small rodents, bear droppings full of berry seeds are like all-you-can-eat buffets. Rummaging through poop for your food might seem gross, but it saves the seed nibblers a lot of time and effort.

After 10 months on the ground, this old bear scat filled with half-digested chokecherries has become a spring garden. The chokecherry seeds are sprouting into reddish seedlings as green grass pushes up around them.
ROB RICH

But rodents can't come close to consuming all the berry seeds grizzlies deposit. The rest remain on the ground, ready to sprout. As the bears wander from one berry patch to the next, they are like farmers sowing future crops.

Grizzlies also act like farmers when they churn up mountain meadows to find roots or bulbs or pursue burrowing rodents. Their digging changes the soil chemistry and gives plants more nitrogen for growing. That increases the food supply for all animals that browse or graze in the meadows.

Each of these contributions is another good reason for us to take care of grizzly bears.

The members of this Youth Conservation Corps crew are all smiles after finishing the hard work of installing a bear-proof food storage box in Yellowstone National Park's Canyon Campground.
JACOB W. FRANK/NPS/FLICKR.COM/PUBLIC DOMAIN

4
CONSERVATION IN ACTION

THE CONSERVATION TOOLBOX

Grizzly-bear conservation presents some big challenges. One is that interactions between grizzlies and humans can be risky for both. For people, the risk of being killed or hurt by a grizzly bear is extremely small. But when interactions turn into conflicts, things usually end badly for the bears. To keep ourselves and grizzly bears secure, we have to do everything we can to avoid potential conflicts.

Another challenge is that it's easy to knock down grizzly-bear numbers and hard to build them back up. The grizzly bear's *reproductive rate* is one of the lowest of any land mammal. A typical female grizzly bear may raise only five cubs to adulthood over her whole lifetime. That's because female grizzlies usually don't become mothers until they are five to eight years old, and they only produce one litter every three to four years. On top of that, grizzly-bear litters are small, and many cubs die within their first year.

Fortunately, grizzly-bear biologists have quite a few tools in their conservation toolbox and are adding new ones all the time.

SANCTUARIES AND SAFE HAVENS

One important tool for grizzly-bear conservation is creating safe spaces for them. These are some of the parks and reserves that make grizzlies their number one priority.

• The Khutzeymateen/K'tzim-a-deen Grizzly Bear Sanctuary in Northern British Columbia safeguards 173 square miles (450 square kilometers) of prime grizzly-bear habitat. Most of it is off-limits to people. Visitors can only get there by boat or floatplane and are not allowed to set foot on land. Instead they board small boats and quietly cruise around the Khutzeymateen *estuary* to watch the grizzlies onshore.

A Khutzeymateen grizzly bear observes a boatload of tourists. Years of carefully regulated bear watching and protection from hunting have taught the local grizzlies that human visitors are not a threat.
JOHN E. MARRIOTT, WILDERNESSPRINTS.COM

- Ni'iinlii Njik (Fishing Branch) Territorial Park in the Yukon protects a very important grizzly-bear feeding site. This part of the Fishing Branch River has an unusual local climate so it keeps flowing even when the air temperature drops below freezing. Each fall dozens of grizzlies gather there during salmon-spawning season. As the grizzlies wade in and out of the river on frigid days, their fur becomes coated with ice.

An "ice bear" fishing in Ni'iinlii Njik (Fishing Branch) Territorial Park in late fall. During this critical feeding time, only a handful of people are allowed to view the grizzlies each day.
JOHN E. MARRIOTT, WILDERNESSPRINTS.COM

- The world's biggest grizzly-bear salmon feasts happen every year in Alaska's McNeil River State Game Sanctuary. Salmon swimming upriver to spawn are slowed down when they reach McNeil River Falls and become easy targets. The grizzlies are amazingly tolerant of each other because there's so much food available. Sometimes they stand almost shoulder to shoulder as they fish. Often 20 or more grizzlies share the falls at one time. The record count is 74.

CONNECTING THE DOTS

When grizzly bears lose habitat, some populations can become isolated or cut off from all the rest. It's like those populations are on islands surrounded by water, except their islands are patches of good grizzly-bear habitat surrounded by ranches, farms, country homes, towns and highways. Bears that venture into those busy areas to find food, mates or a new home face many dangers and may not survive.

Being isolated is worst for small populations. It all comes down to arithmetic—but don't worry if math isn't your thing. The arithmetic of grizzly-bear populations is pretty simple. Bears are added to a population when they are born or move in from other areas. They are subtracted

A mother grizzly bear and her young cubs dodge traffic as they cross a busy highway in the Canadian Rockies.
JOHN E. MARRIOTT, WILDERNESSPRINTS.COM

Surprising Answers to a Camper's Question

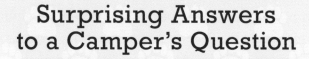

MORGAN HOCKING

Dúqvaísḷá William Housty is the conservation manager for the Heiltsuk Nation's Integrated Resource Management Department. He is also Allie Elluk-Housty's uncle. Like her, William started getting to know grizzly bears while spending time at Koeye Camp. A few years later he was working at the camp when one of the campers asked how many grizzlies were in the area. "Nobody had the slightest clue," William says. So he and the Heiltsuk Nation set out to find the answer.

Their research was guided by the Heiltsuk Ǧviḷás. These customary laws emphasized that the investigations must not disturb the bears. Using barbed wire to snag tufts of hair was the perfect solution.

Partners from several universities and conservation organizations also joined the study. In four years the team collected nearly 800 hair samples from stations they set up along the Koeye River each fall. DNA testing showed that the hair came from 57 different grizzly bears. That was far more than they had expected.

The study highlighted the Koeye River's importance for grizzly bears. It is the southernmost place on the coast where they still gather in large numbers for their annual salmon splurge. Grizzlies used to gather every year along salmon-spawning rivers from northern Alaska all the way down to southern California. Today, fish-filled rivers that support big grizzly-bear populations exist only in Alaska and the northern half of British Columbia.

William and his partners also learned more about where the bears went when they weren't at Koeye. The Koeye hair samples showed that some grizzlies turned up every fall while others would skip a year or two and then reappear. When the researchers started collecting hair in neighboring areas, they discovered that the bears were traveling incredible distances.

"We just couldn't fathom how much they were moving in such a small amount of time," William says. "Some bears covered hundreds of kilometers within a 10-day stretch."

This new knowledge was one reason the Heiltsuk and other First Nations on the north and central coast of British Columbia banned the hunting of bears throughout their territories in 2012. Five years later the government of British Columbia ended grizzly-bear hunting in the whole province.

"I now have a deeper appreciation for how important grizzly bears are. Not only in our culture, but as pieces of the bigger puzzle of the ecosystem, of the territory, of the watershed."
—Dúqvàísḷa William Housty

when they die, move away or are relocated by wildlife managers. A population grows when there are more additions than subtractions. It shrinks when there are more subtractions than additions. If an isolated population is very small, it doesn't take much to send it tumbling to zero.

We can support isolated grizzly-bear populations by making it easier and safer for their members to get off their island when they need to. That starts with reducing their chances of getting hit while crossing roads.

ROAD SAFETY

One way to judge how good an area is for grizzly bears is to count the number of roads running through it, from dirt tracks to multi-lane highways. The more roads there are, the worse it is for bears.

Grizzlies tend to stay away from high-speed traffic, so every busy road in a bear's home range cuts into its useful habitat. But sometimes grizzlies can't avoid roads and are forced to dodge drivers to get to where they need to go. They may even be attracted to these dangerous places to scavenge other animals that have died there or to graze on roadside plants.

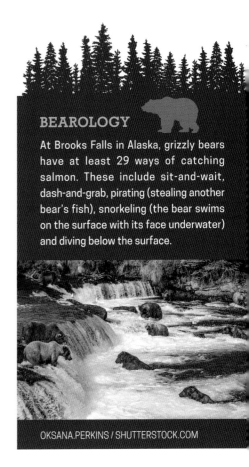

BEAROLOGY

At Brooks Falls in Alaska, grizzly bears have at least 29 ways of catching salmon. These include sit-and-wait, dash-and-grab, pirating (stealing another bear's fish), snorkeling (the bear swims on the surface with its face underwater) and diving below the surface.

OKSANA.PERKINS / SHUTTERSTOCK.COM

Spring is mating season for grizzly bears. Here a determined male follows a female along the Alaska Highway in the Yukon. The people watching them are wisely staying inside their camper.
JOHN E. MARRIOTT, WILDERNESSPRINTS.COM

A wildlife overpass spans the Trans-Canada Highway in Banff National Park. Grizzly bears prefer to use overpasses rather than the more confined underpasses.
MJ_PROTOTYPE/GETTY IMAGES

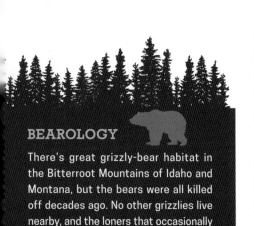

BEAROLOGY

There's great grizzly-bear habitat in the Bitterroot Mountains of Idaho and Montana, but the bears were all killed off decades ago. No other grizzlies live nearby, and the loners that occasionally visit don't stay long because they can't find mates. Biologists who want to return grizzlies to the Bitterroots are studying how to make it safer for more of them to travel there from other areas.

Far too many grizzly bears die after being hit by vehicles. Banff National Park has shown that these deaths are preventable. Within the park, 51 miles (82 kilometers) of fencing keeps wildlife off the busy Trans-Canada Highway. There are also 6 overpasses and 38 underpasses that allow animals to move back and forth across the highway safely.

Since 1997 these fences and crossing structures have saved the lives of dozens of grizzly bears. They have also kept populations on either side of the highway connected. Now other places are following Banff's lead.

The gravel roads and dirt tracks that crisscross much of western North America pose a different problem. Mostly they were built so forestry, mining and oil-and-gas company workers could reach job sites. But they also make it easy for people to get into backcountry areas for recreation.

Grizzly bears don't care whether human intruders are there for work or pleasure. They just want to be left alone. Restricting public use of these roads and shutting them down once they are no longer needed eases the pressure on grizzlies. Both actions are being taken in some places, but grizzly-bear advocates are pushing for more restrictions and closures.

OFF THE TRACKS

Railways are also hazardous for grizzlies. Unfortunately, bears don't always notice oncoming trains or recognize them as a threat. And trains can't slow down quickly or swerve to avoid a collision.

Grizzlies end up on or next to train tracks for various reasons. In some cases they are drawn by food, like grain spilled from railcars or a dead deer, elk or moose that was hit by a train. They also like to take advantage of the easy walking along the tracks.

A grizzly bear that has been feeding on spilled grain eyes an approaching train. Its good view down the tracks will give it enough time to move out of harm's way.
JOHN E. MARRIOTT, WILDERNESSPRINTS.COM

A woman watches as a grizzly-bear mother and cub clamber over a boardwalk by the historic Old Faithful Inn in Yellowstone National Park.

JIM PEACO/YELLOWSTONE NATIONAL PARK/ FLICKR.COM/PUBLIC DOMAIN

Railway companies and wildlife managers are trying to keep bears off the tracks by cleaning up grain spills and removing carcasses as quickly as possible. They are also trying to make life safer for the grizzlies that continue to loiter around rail lines. In some places they are cutting trackside vegetation so bears can spot approaching trains sooner and have more time to escape. In others they are clearing trails that run parallel to the tracks and serve as wildlife sidewalks.

Grizzly bears remain at risk in places where they can't see trains coming around curves or can't hear them because they are near a rushing river. A recent invention might be the solution. It's a small black box that can be attached to train tracks in any problem area. Magnetic and vibration sensors detect trains 30 seconds before they arrive and trigger flashing lights and loud beeps. Trials have shown that the warnings send nearby grizzlies scampering, so the boxes may soon come into common use.

NO MORE FREE LUNCHES FOR YOGI

If you had visited Yellowstone National Park back in the old days, watching bears eat garbage might have been the highlight of your trip. Really! Throughout the first half of the 20th century, the park's hotels and restaurants pitched their waste into open pits. Crowds gathered at these dumps every evening to watch grizzly and black bears paw through the piles and brawl over the best food scraps. A few sites had bleachers where spectators could sit and enjoy the entertainment. While the tourists observed the action, park rangers gave educational talks.

Lots of North American parks had these kinds of garbage cafeterias for bears, with public viewing areas, but Yellowstone was the most famous. Visitors to many parks also fed bears along roadsides. Some tossed treats from their car windows. Others boldly approached the animals and held out offerings. The bears quickly learned to connect people with food. Soon they were helping themselves to snacks from cars, campgrounds and picnic sites—just like Yogi Bear, the cartoon character who lives in a made-up place called Jellystone National Park and constantly tries to steal picnic baskets.

A bear-feeding station in Yellowstone National Park in the 1920s or 1930s. Bears came to this "lunch counter" for easy meals. Tourists came to gawk and snap pictures.
UNKNOWN PHOTOGRAPHER/YELLOWSTONE NATIONAL PARK/FLICKR.COM/PUBLIC DOMAIN

Even the most persistent bear can't open the lids of these bear-proof garbage cans.
T. SCHNEIDER/SHUTTERSTOCK.COM

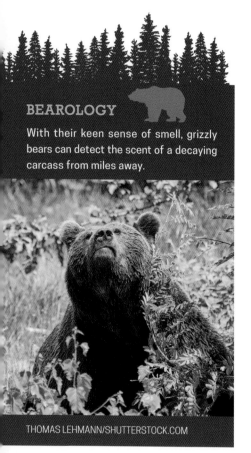

BEAROLOGY

With their keen sense of smell, grizzly bears can detect the scent of a decaying carcass from miles away.

THOMAS LEHMANN/SHUTTERSTOCK.COM

In the 1940s Yellowstone was one of the first parks to stop staging bear shows. But it still had some garbage dumps where bears went to eat and people went to see them. In 1970 Yellowstone finally shut down its last open-pit dump and installed bear-proof garbage bins throughout the park. The park also banned all feeding of bears. No more handouts. No more leaving edibles in empty campsites, open vehicles or anywhere else that bears could reach. No more free lunches for Yogi and his buddies. Those rules are now standard in all parks where there are bears and in many other places where bears and people share the landscape.

TIPPING OVER TRASH CANS

Once grizzly bears learn where to find goodies, they keep coming back for more. They also look for similar sources of food. These behaviors are essential for surviving in the natural world, but cause problems when the food comes from people.

The human world is full of potential bear foods. They include anything we eat, anything edible that we throw away and any food we put out for pets, livestock or wild birds. Grizzly bears don't just raid picnic tables and tip over trash cans. They also climb fruit trees to harvest the ripe fruit. They tear open beehives to get honey and bee *larvae*. They bust into grain bins and raid corn fields. And sometimes they kill domestic animals, such as calves, lambs or chickens. As far as they're concerned, it's all fair game. But these activities can be costly and upsetting for the people involved.

A grizzly bear peers into a culvert trap, drawn by the smelly bait inside. Culvert traps are use to capture troublemakers without hurting them. Once the door slams shut, the bear can be temporarily put to sleep and moved to another location.
GRANT MACHUTCHON

SECOND CHANCES AND SAD ENDINGS

When wildlife managers decide a bear is doing too much damage to human property or is a threat to human safety, they act quickly. Often they take the bear far away and release it. Relocation gives bears a second chance, but it's tough on them. First there's the scary experience of being trapped and drugged and waking up in a foreign land. Then the relocated bear has to find food while avoiding bears that already live in the area. After a lifetime of getting to know its own home range, it suddenly has to figure out how to survive in unfamiliar surroundings. Some relocated bears do well in their new homes. Many do not.

RESCUE/RELEASE IN PROGRESS

for more info
www.wildlifeshelter.com

This lucky grizzly bear was rescued as a cub and cared for at the Northern Lights Wildlife Shelter. Now it is on its way to a new home in the wild.
JOHN E. MARRIOTT, WILDERNESSPRINTS.COM

Sometimes it isn't even possible to relocate bears because there is no suitable place for them. A new location has to have room for an additional bear. It also has to be a long way from the bear's original home so it can't make a beeline back to its old address. And it should be free of the kind of temptations the bear was hooked on. Relocation is also not an option for repeat offenders or very aggressive bears.

Wildlife managers want to keep wildlife alive. Sadly, when they cannot move a bear they nearly always have to kill it. If they are lucky, they might be able to find a place for the bear in a zoo or wildlife refuge. But that's never as good as living free. Instead of making bears pay a penalty for their behavior, it's better to help them steer clear of conflicts.

Most orphaned grizzly-bear cubs spend the rest of their lives in captivity. Other grizzlies end up in zoos because they have used up their last chances or there is nowhere to release them.
JAMES NGUYEN1/SHUTTERSTOCK.COM

An electric fence around this Yukon campsite keeps bears from trespassing.
JOHN E. MARRIOTT, WILDERNESSPRINTS.COM

BACK OFF, BEAR!

Being quick to learn about *people food* gets grizzlies into a lot of trouble. Their smarts can also help them learn to avoid trouble. There are several ways to teach bears to stay away from us and our food. They all aim to give the bear an unpleasant—but not harmful—experience that it won't want to repeat.

Electric fences can put all kinds of places out of bounds, including gardens, orchards, grain silos, chicken coops, beehives, livestock corrals, barnyards and camp-sites. The moment a bear makes contact with the fence, it gets a jolt that makes it slam on the brakes and jump back. One shock is usually enough. The pain doesn't last long, but the memory of it does.

Wildlife managers sometimes tell bears to back off by shooting beanbags or rubber bullets at them. Bangers or crackers that are shot from a gun and explode loudly in midair are also good for convincing bears they're not welcome.

After demolishing these plastic garbage bins and snacking on the contents, the grizzly bear that did this damage is sure to return for more.
JOHN E. MARRIOTT, WILDERNESSPRINTS.COM

One of the Wind River Bear Institute's Karelian bear dogs on the job, chasing an American black bear. These trained dogs and their handlers work with all three North American bear species and with Asian black bears in Japan.
JOHN T. HUMPHREY

A Yellowstone National Park Youth Conservation Corps crew hefts a bear-proof food-storage box into place. These heavy steel containers help keep bears out of trouble and ensure camper safety.
YELLOWSTONE NATIONAL PARK/ FLICKR.COM/ PUBLIC DOMAIN

Another way to make an effective bear-scaring commotion is with a trained Karelian bear dog—or KBD for short. KBDs are hunting dogs that originated in Finland and are fearless around bears. Biologist Carrie Hunt brought the first Karelian bear dogs to North America in the 1990s and founded the Wind River Bear Institute in Montana. She and her team train the dogs to work with bears that have learned problem-causing habits. They currently have about 10 working dogs. They also breed the dogs and teach people how to be KBD handlers.

Karelian bear dogs don't attack bears, and they stay clear of their opponent's claws and teeth. They do their job by dashing around barking at the bear and annoying it so much that it gets fed up and runs away. After a brush with a KBD and its handler, most bears want nothing more to do with either dogs or humans.

Two orphaned grizzly-bear cubs play together in a pen at the Northern Lights Wildlife Shelter. Once they are old enough to survive on their own, they will be returned to the wild.
JOHN E. MARRIOTT, WILDERNESSPRINTS.COM

CUB CARE

The unnatural death of any grizzly bear is a loss for the species. It's even worse if that bear is the mother of young cubs. Most orphaned grizzlies either die or spend the rest of their lives in captivity. Either way, the wild population ends up poorer.

Many kinds of orphaned animals can be cared for in wildlife rescue centers and then released once they can fend for themselves. Dealing with grizzly-bear cubs is more difficult because they normally stay with their mothers until they are two or three years old. They need that time to grow big enough and learn enough to survive on their own. The problem is that it's hard to take care of cubs for two or three years without them getting used to being around people. And when grizzly bears become too familiar with humans, they can't be set free.

Smile for the Camera

Biologist Melanie Clapham spends a lot of time observing grizzly bears and often sees the same individuals more than once. But she doesn't always recognize them because most grizzlies don't have distinctive markings. Even when Melanie gets to know a particular bear, she can't count on its appearance staying the same.

A grizzly that you see in May can look like a completely different bear in August. The transformation can be caused by a huge weight gain or by changes in the bear's fur color as it sheds its heavy winter coat in spring and its new coat grows in.

A few years ago Melanie started studying grizzly-bear scent marking. She placed trail cameras near rub trees to take photos and record videos of grizzlies that visited the trees. But to properly understand their behavior, she needed to be able to tell them apart. She decided to see if computers could help.

Melanie soon discovered that a couple of software developers named Ed Miller and Mary Nguyen were working on a similar idea. The three teamed up and designed a computer application called BearID.

BearID uses a type of artificial intelligence known as deep learning to analyze images of grizzly bears. First the application scans the image to find the bear's face and zero in on certain features, such as the eyes and the tip of the nose. Next it creates a close-up picture and examines it to figure out what is unique about that bear's face. The application then turns that information into a number code.

Once a picture of a bear's face has been tagged with numbers, BearID can compare it to all the others it has examined. When two faces have closely matching numbers, Melanie knows they are photos of the same bear. If no other face has a matching number, it's possibly a new bear. Two bears may look alike to the human eye, but the computer can spot the differences.

MOIRA LE PATOUREL

"If we can recognize individual grizzlies we can study them throughout their lives. We can also estimate how many bears live in an area and whether their numbers are going up or down."
—Melanie Clapham

One wildlife center in Northern British Columbia has figured out how to look after motherless grizzly-bear cubs so they can be safely returned to the wild. It is the only facility in North America that is allowed to rescue and release orphaned grizzlies.

The Northern Lights Wildlife Shelter was founded by Angelika and Peter Langen. They are both trained animal keepers who worked in zoos in Germany before they immigrated to Canada. Since 2007 they have given more than 18 grizzly-bear orphans a fresh start. Angelika and Peter make sure the cubs have very little contact with people before they get to the shelter and while they are there. When they release them, they choose wilderness locations where the bears will be able to find lots of good natural foods and aren't likely to happen across any humans.

Originally there was no way of knowing the fate of the Northern Lights bears after they were released. Now biologists are tracking the orphans to see if they go on to lead successful lives in the wild. If they can prove that this approach to rescuing orphaned grizzly bears works, it will become another important tool in the grizzly-bear conservation toolbox.

BearID software developer Mary Nguyen at work. Melanie Clapham met her and Ed Miller through Wildlabs, an online community of conservation scientists, computer specialists and technology experts who work together to solve conservation problems around the world.
ED MILLER

A face-detection image produced by the BearID computer application.
MELANIE CLAPHAM

A grizzly bear wanders through a campground filled with enticing smells.
JOHN E. MARRIOTT, WILDERNESSPRINTS.COM

5

GRIZZLY BEARS AND YOU

EVERYONE CAN CONTRIBUTE

Grizzly bears are quite adaptable. In places where they live close to people, some grizzlies adapt by carrying out more of their activities at night than during the day. Operating after dark helps them avoid risky interactions with people, but those grizzlies still lead dangerous lives. Like bears that are active in the daytime, nocturnal bears can develop a fondness for people food. And highways are even more treacherous at night than during the day.

Humans are also adaptable, and we have more options for changing our ways than animals do. If you live in or visit areas where there are grizzly bears, talk to your family about what you can do together to safely coexist with grizzlies and keep them around. Also remember that you don't have to be in the grizzly bear's backyard to support this species.

Gifts for Grizzlies

Wisconsin was never home to wild grizzlies, but it is home to a special stuffed toy grizzly bear named Murray. He lives with Kloe Johnson and inspired her generous support of grizzlies in the northwestern United States. Murray originally belonged to Kloe's father. The large, huggable bear became hers when she was eight and got

sick at Christmastime. The two spent a lot of that holiday cuddled up together.

As time went on, Kloe became curious about what Murray's life would be like if he were a real bear. She started doing research and learning about things like hibernation and what grizzlies eat. Kloe loves climbing trees, so one of her favorite discoveries was that grizzly-bear cubs are tree climbers too—although in their case it's usually to escape danger.

Kloe also learned that grizzly bears are losing habitat in certain areas and grizzlies that live near humans often end up being killed. "I wanted to do something to help members of Murray's family," she says. So she decided to use her 10th birthday to raise money for a grizzly-bear conservation organization. After some more research she settled on the Vital Ground Foundation. Its goals are to protect grizzly-bear habitat and reduce conflicts between grizzlies and humans.

For her birthday sleepover, Kloe chose a Harry Potter theme. Her stepmother created the invitations. They looked like Hogwarts Express train tickets and read *No Gifts, Please! Mr. Murray is collecting donations on behalf of fellow grizzly bears*. It was a small party—just Kloe and her three best friends—but the fundraiser was a success.

That Christmas Kloe repeated her request for donations instead of presents, and Vital Ground Foundation received more money for their grizzly-bear conservation work.

Kloe has yet to see a grizzly bear in the wild. "I'd like to see one," she says, "but from a distance!" For now she has Murray at her side, encouraging her to stand up for his real-life relatives out west.

> "Grizzly-bear conservation is important because more and more people are moving into some of the places where they live."
> —Kloe Johnson

(TOP AND BOTTOM) ANNA GARDNER

A resident of the Grizzly & Wolf Discovery Center in West Yellowstone, MT, tests a garbage can. If it can't open the container and get the food that is inside within one hour, the Interagency Grizzly Bear Committee will certify it as bear-resistant.
GRIZZLY & WOLF DISCOVERY CENTER

ELIMINATE TEMPTATIONS

When grizzlies get into people's bad books they are often labeled as problem bears. But the real problem is usually that people put temptations in their path.

Those temptations are called attractants because they attract the attention of hungry bears. Grizzlies rely heavily on their noses to find food and will investigate all kinds of odors. A tube of sunscreen might turn out to taste terrible, but a bear won't know that until it has tried eating it. Grizzlies also search for meals with their eyes and learn where to look. For example, once a bear realizes that coolers usually contain food, it will check out any cooler it sees.

Whether you are at home or out camping, being a good neighbor to bears starts with identifying potential attractants. The next step is to get rid of them or put them completely out of reach. Some bear-proofing projects—like installing electric fences—need to be done by adults. But kids can play a big role in eliminating temptations for bears.

BEAROLOGY

It's challenging for any grizzly bear to survive in areas dominated by humans, but subadults have the worst survival rate. Four decades of research from British Columbia show that for every young grizzly that learned how to live a healthy and peaceful life around people, 29 others met an early death.

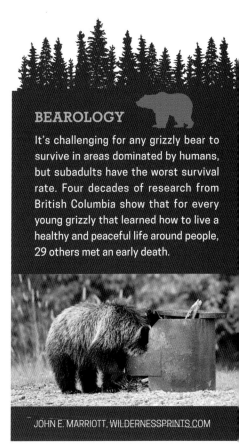

JOHN E. MARRIOTT, WILDERNESSPRINTS.COM

BEAR-PROOFING ACTIONS AT HOME AND AWAY

Around your home, you could take responsibility for activities such as:

• putting out your family's garbage cans on the morning of pickup and returning them to their secure storage place before nighttime;

• making sure pet-food bowls aren't left sitting around outside and that pet-food containers are stored securely;

• picking the fruit from trees in your yard as it ripens and collecting fallen fruit from the ground every day;

• bringing in your Halloween pumpkin at night and, after Halloween, disposing of your pumpkin in a way that won't attract bears;

• being on clean-up patrol so no smelly items like food wrappers and empty drink cans get left in your family's car.

When camping, it's important to keep a bare campsite—not a bear campsite—so bears don't drop in when you are away or sleeping. Two key things you can help with are:

• taking garbage and recyclable containers to the campground's bear proof bins after every meal and before you go to bed;

• putting attractants inside a vehicle or bear-proof storage locker whenever no one is going to be in camp and before bedtime. Attractants are not just food and garbage. They include anything that has been used to prepare, cook, consume or store food and drinks, as well as scented stuff like toothpaste, deodorant and insect repellent.

A bear jam along a highway in the Canadian Rockies. Most of these people are not following the guidelines for watching roadside bears safely and respectfully.
JOHN E. MARRIOTT, WILDERNESSPRINTS.COM

RESPECT ROADSIDE BEARS

Most of us don't regularly see wild grizzly bears, so we get excited whenever we spot one. I certainly do. Often these sightings happen when we are driving. Open areas next to roads are like salad bars for grizzlies in spring and early summer. It's hard to resist stopping to watch them graze on the greenery and tear off mouthfuls of dandelion and clover blossoms.

If roadside viewing is done wrong, it's risky for everyone. When drivers slow down or stop to gawk, there's a danger of car accidents, and bears or people on the road may get hit. Sometimes so many cars stop in one place to watch bears, they cause a "bear jam."

Being crowded by people is also stressful for bears. Imagine trying to eat your lunch with a bunch of curious strangers staring at you. When bears get too uncomfortable, they usually retreat and lose out on a good meal. Occasionally they take a run at the spectators.

A grizzly bear dashes across a road in Yellowstone National Park while a ranger controls traffic and keeps the bear watchers from getting too close.
ERIC JOHNSTON/NPS PHOTO

So what's the right way to view roadside bears? Here are some guidelines.

• Only stop if the driver can safely pull over and park on the shoulder. Don't get mad if they decide to keep going because there's no place to stop or too much traffic. Sometimes you have to be content with just a glimpse of a roadside bear as you go by.

• If you do stop, it should be at a respectful distance from the bear—at least 100 yards (91 meters). The more space we give bears, the less stress we cause them.

• Everyone should stay in the vehicle. You will be safer, and the bear will be less bothered.

• If the bear seems comfortable, watch from the car for a few minutes and maybe take a few pictures. Then move on.

Trying to feed a roadside bear is obviously a no-no. If one approaches your vehicle while you are stopped, honk the horn, close the windows and drive away immediately. If you stick around, the bear will get more used to people, and that may shorten its life.

STAY SAFE ON THE TRAIL

Grizzly bears live in some of the most beautiful parts of North America. If we want to explore those places, we need to go prepared to make it a safe experience for ourselves and any grizzlies that are around. Kids should always take along some adults when they go out on the trail in grizzly-bear country. But it's good for everyone in the group to know about bear safety, not just the adults.

A line of tracks in the mud records a grizzly bear's journey. The natural walking speed for grizzlies is about 1.3 miles (2 kilometers) per hour. Humans walk at a similar speed.
GLACIER BAY NATIONAL PARK AND PRESERVE/ NPS PHOTO

Here are a few important rules to keep in mind:

- The larger your group, the safer you will be. The recommended minimum number of people for hiking in grizzly-bear country is three.

- Stick together, with the smallest people in the middle of the pack.

- The adults should carry **bear spray** and know how to use it. Older kids who have had bear-spray training can also carry a canister.

- If you bring a dog with you, keep it leashed at all times. A dog that is running free and upsets a bear can bring trouble with it when it dashes back to its owners.

A kid practices shooting fake bear spray at a plywood bear as it speeds forward on a wheeled track. Bear-safety training events like this one prepare people for adventures in bear country.
JACOB W. FRANK/NPS/FLICKR.COM/
PUBLIC DOMAIN

With the smallest person in the middle, a group of hikers treks along the Bunsen Peak Trail in Yellowstone National Park. This trail passes through forest and meadows. Grizzly bears are common in the area.
JIM PEACO/YELLOWSTONE NATIONAL PARK/
FLICKR.COM/PUBLIC DOMAIN

Rowan Sharman stands by a grizzly-bear stomp trail during a backpacking trip along the outer coast of Glacier Bay National Park and Preserve. The bear-spray canister attached to his belt is easy to reach if he needs it.
LEWIS SHARMAN

A young naturalist and a park ranger investigate a pile of bear scat on a trail.
GLACIER BAY NATIONAL PARK AND PRESERVE/ NPS PHOTO

- Grizzly bears normally avoid people if they smell, hear or see them in time to move away. Make lots of noise so you won't take them by surprise, especially if you're walking into the wind. Sing songs and talk loudly. In places where the visibility is poor, call out to announce your presence. I like to shout, "Hey, bear! Coming through!" Or "Helloooo, bears!"

- Don't hike at dawn or dusk or during the night. Those are the times when grizzly bears are most active.

- Pay constant attention to your surroundings. Watch for bear tracks, scat, diggings and other signs. When grizzlies kill or scavenge an animal that is too big to eat all at once, they stay nearby and guard that food until they have finished it off. They often cover the remains with dirt or brush. If you smell or see a dead animal or notice a gathering of birds like ravens or magpies, don't go any closer. Instead go back the way you came. If that's not possible, make a wide detour.

- If you are mountain biking in bear country, slow down. Cyclists travel much faster than people on foot, so they are more likely to surprise a bear. They are also more likely to zip around a corner and collide with an unsuspecting bear. Not surprisingly, bears don't take kindly to that kind of rudeness.

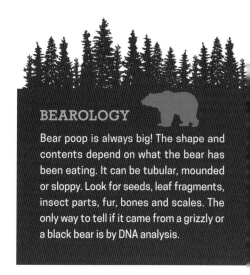

BEAROLOGY

Bear poop is always big! The shape and contents depend on what the bear has been eating. It can be tubular, mounded or sloppy. Look for seeds, leaf fragments, insect parts, fur, bones and scales. The only way to tell if it came from a grizzly or a black bear is by DNA analysis.

BE A GOOD GUEST

If you do come across a grizzly bear while you're on the trail, stay calm. If the bear seems unaware of your group, try to move away quietly without getting its attention. If it has already spotted you, politely identify yourselves as humans. Talk to it in respectful voices and slowly wave your arms. Then gradually move away without turning your back on the bear. Never run, because running may prompt the bear to chase you.

The idea of going out into grizzly-bear country can make people nervous or even downright scared. Rather than fueling your fear with thoughts of hostile bears, try to think of yourself as a guest in the grizzly's home—and aim to be a good one. Give any bears you see the space they need and deserve. If you get to the trailhead and discover a sign saying the trail is closed because of bear activity, find somewhere else to hike. If bears are feeding in a berry patch where you wanted to pick, let them have it to them- selves. And always be willing to turn around and retrace your steps if you have to.

JACOB W. FRANK/NPS PHOTO

A couple of wet grizzlies plod along a dirt road in Denali National Park and Preserve during a late-summer snowfall.
NPS PHOTO

Students from Bella Bella Community School in British Columbia learn about grizzly and black bears during a field trip to a Raincoast Conservation Foundation research site. The researchers have strung barbed wire to snag bear hair and mounted a trail camera on a tree.
JOHANNA GORDON-WALKER

COMBAT CLIMATE CHANGE

Summers are getting longer, hotter and drier in much of western North America, and these changes are hitting some grizzly bears where it hurts most—right in the stomach. Salmon eaters are among the most affected because many Pacific salmon populations are collapsing. When fewer salmon return from the ocean to spawn, grizzlies suffer. So do all the animals and plants that benefit from the salmon scraps and scat that grizzly bears spread around.

Climate change is also affecting berries and the grizzlies that rely on them. Plants that don't get enough moisture produce fewer and smaller berries. Another problem is that berries are ripening earlier than they used to in many places. The longer gap between berry season and winter means grizzlies may enter hibernation with less body fat.

Training and a Cool Head Pay Off

JAN AALT VAN DEN HOORN

William van den Hoorn lives in a rural part of the southern Yukon. Growing up, he always knew there were grizzly bears around, and every few years he would see one. But those sightings were nothing like the close encounter he had when he was 14.

That May afternoon William and his dogs, Oscar and Orca, were out for a walk along a quiet road near his home. About half a mile (0.8 kilometers) from the house, he paused at the top of a hill. Suddenly Oscar began barking and growling at something behind William's back.

"I turned around and there was a huge grizzly walking toward me," William recalls. "I was pretty shocked." At that point the bear was about 33 yards (30 meters) away.

William's bear-safety training—from outdoor school activities and family conversations—immediately kicked into action. He started slowly backing away while waving his arms and talking loudly. But the curious bear wasn't fazed. "It wasn't showing any aggression," he says. "It just wouldn't stop coming."

Before leaving home, William had done what he always does. He had grabbed the bear-spray canister his family keeps near the door. As the distance between him and the grizzly narrowed, he pulled the canister from its holster, flipped off the safety clip and got ready to press the trigger. William had once practiced with a canister of fake bear spray during an outdoor-education program. He knew if he fired too soon, the spray would fall short of his target.

The grizzly was only 5.5 yards (5 meters) away when William let loose. The blast hit it full in the face, and the bear wheeled around and fled into the forest. William waited warily until it was completely out of sight. Then he and the dogs hightailed it for home. They were shaken but safe, and so was the grizzly bear.

> "We are super proud of William for
> the way he handled himself."
> —William's mother, Fiona van den Hoorn

BEAROLOGY

Think you can outrun a grizzly bear? Think again! Grizzlies can run very fast for short distances—up to 35 miles (56 kilometers) per hour. The human sprinting speed record is 23 miles (37 kilometers) per hour.

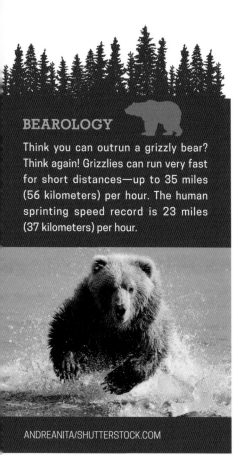

ANDREANITA/SHUTTERSTOCK.COM

Mother grizzly bears work hard to take care of their cubs. Our efforts can also help give them a safe and healthy future.
VOLODYMYR BURDIAK/SHUTTERSTOCK.COM

Grizzly bears that eat whitebark-pine seeds are losing another important food. Over the past few decades, climate change has killed huge numbers of whitebark pines. These trees grow extremely slowly. Any new ones that manage to sprout won't get big enough to produce seeds for many years.

Fortunately, when one item is struck off the menu, grizzly bears can usually find something else to eat. This flexibility is helping them cope with climate change. But switching to different foods can come at a cost. Bears that have to spend more time looking for food or settle for less-nutritious options can find it hard to maintain a healthy weight. And if they turn to people foods to try to make up for the shortage of natural foods, they usually pay a high price.

Biologists are also concerned about the effects of climate change on hibernation patterns. Grizzly bears don't use alarm clocks. Their wake-up time is mostly based on the outside temperature. So in places where spring is arriving sooner than it used to, grizzlies are emerging from their dens earlier.

Being an early riser can be good for grizzlies because it gives them more time for eating. But it also increases the number of days in the year that they are at risk from run-ins with people. Shorter hibernation may be worst for first-year cubs because they head out into the world when they are smaller and more vulnerable.

There are many ways each of us can combat climate change. Simple actions you can take include things like putting on a sweater when you're cold instead of turning up the heat in your home and cutting down on car trips by walking, biking or taking the bus whenever possible.

LEARN AND SHARE

Above all, if you want to help grizzly bears, keep learning about them and sharing your knowledge with friends, relatives and members of your community. Let them know why grizzly bears are important and how they too can lend a hand, whether that's through working on coexistence or supporting habitat protection or both.

As guardians of the wilderness, grizzly bears make the world a better place for every one of us. We can each do our part to make the world a better place for them.

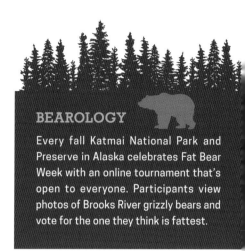

BEAROLOGY

Every fall Katmai National Park and Preserve in Alaska celebrates Fat Bear Week with an online tournament that's open to everyone. Participants view photos of Brooks River grizzly bears and vote for the one they think is fattest.

A family pays close attention as a US Forest Service employee explains the differences between black and grizzly bears. The bear facing the camera is a black bear. The one facing away is a grizzly.
JACOB W. FRANK/NPS/FLICKR.COM/
PUBLIC DOMAIN

GLOSSARY

alpine—the high mountain zone above the limit of where trees can grow

apex predator—an animal that hunts and eats other animals but is not hunted and eaten by any other predator, except humans in some cases

bear spray—a spray for repelling aggressive bears, which contains the same chemicals that make chili peppers so hot

biodiversity—the variety of all living things

DNA—coded molecules found in every cell of every living thing to provide instructions for development, growth and reproduction. DNA stands for deoxyribonucleic acid.

ecosystem—a community of living things, along with the nonliving parts of their environment (such as water, soil and rocks), all linked together through nutrient cycles and energy flows

estuary—the area where a river meets the ocean and fresh water mixes with salt water

euthanize—to kill an animal painlessly, usually by giving it a drug that causes it to lose consciousness

GPS—a navigation system that uses satellite signals to determine the ground position of an object. GPS stands for Global Positioning System.

guard hairs—long, coarse outer hairs that protect the grizzly bear's softer underfur

habitat—the place where a plant or animal makes its home and can get all the things it needs to survive, such as food, water and shelter

hibernation—a state of inactivity in winter during which the hibernating animal's body temperature drops and its breathing and heart rate slow down

home range—the area in which an individual animal travels in its search for all the things it needs, including food and mates

hyperphagia—the extreme eating that grizzly bears do to fatten up before they start hibernating

inland—the area far from the ocean and coast

invertebrates—animals that have no backbone or spinal column

larvae—a group of hatched insects in their first stage of life. Larvae are wingless and often wormlike.

logjam—a jumble of logs wedged together in a stream or river

Lower 48 states—the part of the continental United States that lies south of the Canadian border. It includes all US states except Alaska and Hawaii.

people food—anything bears will eat that is not part of their natural diet and is associated with people

population—all the individuals of one species that live in a particular area

reproductive rate—the average number of offspring that females of a particular species produce during their lifetime

scat—digested wastes deposited by animals

scavenge—the act of feeding on garbage or a dead animal

spawning—the period in which female fish deposit their eggs and male fish fertilize them

species—a group of closely related organisms that have similar characteristics and can breed to produce offspring

subspecies—a subgroup within a species. Different subspecies within a species usually live apart from one another.

trail camera—a camera that is placed outside and left there to take photos or videos when it is triggered by passing animals

tundra—a vast area of flatland in the Arctic where it is too cold, dry and windy for trees to grow and the main plants are tough grasses, mosses, lichens and low shrubs

umbrella species—an animal whose required habitat stretches out over the habitats of many other animals and plants, so when its habitat is protected, those other species also benefit

RESOURCES

PRINT

Busch, Robert H. *The Grizzly Almanac*. Fitzhenry & Whiteside, 2000.

Craighead, Lance. *Bears of the World*. Voyageur Press, 2000.

Masterson, Linda. *Living With Bears Handbook*. PixyJack Press, 2016.

McAllister, Ian, and Nicholas Read. *The Salmon Bears: Giants of the Great Bear Rainforest*. Orca Book Publishers, 2010.

Van Tighem, Kevin. *Bears Without Fear*. Rocky Mountain Books, 2013.

VIDEO

Bears: A Yellowstone Love Story. On the YellowstoneNPS YouTube channel.

Dance in British Columbia: Evoking the Wild Grizzly Bear's Spirit (featuring Laura Grizzlypaws). On the New York Times YouTube channel.

Defenders: A Day in the Life—Monitoring for Bears in the Bitterroot. On the Defenders of Wildlife YouTube channel.

Middle School Scientists: Glacier Bay Bears. Produced by the National Park Service.

Sharing the Range (farmers and ranchers coexisting with grizzly bears). On the Waterton Biosphere Reserve YouTube channel.

St'át'imc Nation Grizzly Bear Translocation Project. On the Statimc Govt YouTube channel.

These Bears Put Your Household Items to the Test (grizzlies testing food containers and garbage cans for bear-resistant product certification). On the Great Big Story YouTube channel.

ONLINE

All Grizzly Natural History: allgrizzly.org

Bear Butter (grizzly bears and army cutworm moths): bearbutter.org

BearID Project: bearresearch.org

Coast to Cascades Grizzly Bear Initiative: coasttocascades.org

Fat Bear Week (including a link to Fat Bear Week in the Classroom): explore.org/
    fat-bear-week

Get Bear Smart Society: bearsmart.com

Grizzly & Wolf Discovery Center: grizzlyctr.givecloud.co

Grizzly Bear Foundation: grizzlybearfoundation.com

Hinterland Who's Who—Grizzly Bear: hww.ca/en/wildlife/mammals/grizzly-bear.html

Interagency Grizzly Bear Committee: igbconline.org

International Association for Bear Research and Management: bearbiology.org

Katmai Bear Cams (livestreaming): nps.gov/katm/learn/photosmultimedia/webcams.htm

National Park Service—Bears: nps.gov/subjects/bears

Northern Lights Wildlife Shelter: wildlifeshelter.com

Parks Canada—Bears in the mountain national parks: pc.gc.ca/en/pn-np/mtn/ours-bears

Raincoast Conservation Foundation: raincoast.org/projects/grizzly-bears

South Rockies Grizzly Bear Project: grizzlyresearch.ca

Trans-border Grizzly Bear Project: transbordergrizzlybearproject.ca

US Fish and Wildlife Service—Grizzly Bear: fws.gov/mountain-prairie/es/grizzlyBear.php

Vital Ground Foundation: vitalground.org

Washington State University Bear Center: bearcenter.wsu.edu

Wind River Bear Institute: beardogs.org

Yellowstone to Yukon Conservation Initiative: y2y.net

Links to external resources are for personal and/or educational use only and are provided in good faith without any express or implied warranty. There is no guarantee given as to the accuracy or currency of any individual item. The author and publisher provide links as a service to readers. This does not imply any endorsement by the author or publisher of any of the content accessed through these links.

For other educational resources, visit the page for this book at orcabook.com.

ACKNOWLEDGMENTS

This book draws on the collected knowledge and wisdom of generations of people who have learned about grizzly bears from many different perspectives, including members of Indigenous communities, biologists, citizen scientists and bear-country residents.

For specific assistance in my research for the text and photos, I thank Margaret Seguin Anderson, Kyle Artelle, Melanie Clapham, Chris Darimont, Roberta Edzerza, Jennifer Fortin-Noreus, Cayce Foster, Reba France, Johanna Gordon-Walker, Karen Graham, Crystal Hiebert, Juanita Johnston, Heather Keepers, Emily Kosakowski, Clayton Lamb, Angelika Langen, Grant MacHutchon, John Marriott, Emily McLennan, Renee Miller, Danielle Oyler, Nils Pedersen, Erik Peterson, Rob Rich, Danielle Rivet, Charles Robbins, Sean Tevebaugh, the Ts'msyen Sm'algya̱x Language Authority and Linda Veress.

Special thanks to Jennifer Fortin-Noreus and Grant MacHutchon, who both patiently answered many questions and took the time to read and comment on early drafts of the book. I also greatly appreciated Melanie Clapham's and Clayton Lamb's reviews of specific sections. All the feedback I received from my first readers was valuable, and any errors in the book are mine.

I am deeply grateful to those who told me their personal grizzly-bear stories and gave me permission to share them here. Many thanks to Allie Elluk-Housty, Laura Grizzlypaws, Bryce Hennings, Dúqvàísḷa William Housty, Kloe Johnson, Clayton Lamb and William van den Hoorn. And for their help in connecting me with these storytellers, thanks to Annette Belke, Adam Danis, Anna Gardner, Johanna Gordon-Walker, Tatum McConnell, Gordon Stenhouse and Fiona van den Hoorn.

The British Columbia Arts Council contributed to my work on *Grizzly Bears* with a Project Assistance for Creative Writers grant.

It was a pleasure to work again with Kirstie Hudson and the rest of the wonderful Orca Book Publishers team. I'm lucky to have had such expertise and encouragement throughout the process of creating this book and sending it out into the world. Thanks also to Carolyn Swayze, my literary agent, for laying the groundwork.

And last but certainly not least, big bear hugs to Mark Zuehlke for his steadfast love, support and home cooking.

INDEX

*Page numbers in **bold** indicate an image caption.*

MARK ZUEHLKE

FRANCES BACKHOUSE studied biology in university and worked as a park naturalist and a biologist before becoming an environmental journalist and author. She is the author of *Beavers: Radical Rodents and Ecosystem Engineers* and six books for adults, including *Children of the Klondike*. Camping is one of Frances's favorite ways to spend time outdoors. In bear country she is extra careful to keep a clean campsite so she doesn't invite in any unwelcome wildlife visitors. Frances lives in Victoria, British Columbia.